W9-CAO-966

**OPPOSING
VIEWPOINTS®
SERIES**

Netiquette and Online Ethics

Other Books of Related Interest:

"Congress shall make no law . . . abridging the freedom of speech, or of the press."

First Amendment to the US Constitution

The basic foundation of our democracy is the First Amendment guarantee of freedom of expression. The Opposing Viewpoints series is dedicated to the concept of this basic freedom and the idea that it is more important to practice it than to enshrine it.

OPPOSING
VIEWPOINTS®
SERIES

Netiquette and Online Ethics

Noah Berlatsky, Book Editor

GREENHAVEN PRESS
A part of Gale, Cengage Learning

GALE
CENGAGE Learning·

Detroit • New York • San Francisco • New Haven, Conn • Waterville, Maine • London

Elizabeth Des Chenes, *Director, Publishing Solutions*

© 2013 Greenhaven Press, a part of Gale, Cengage Learning.

Gale and Greenhaven Press are registered trademarks used herein under license.

For more information, contact:
Greenhaven Press
27500 Drake Rd.
Farmington Hills, MI 48331-3535
Or you can visit our Internet site at gale.cengage.com

ALL RIGHTS RESERVED.
No part of this work covered by the copyright herein may be reproduced, transmitted, stored, or used in any form or by any means graphic, electronic, or mechanical, including but not limited to photocopying, recording, scanning, digitizing, taping, Web distribution, information networks, or information storage and retrieval systems, except as permitted under Section 107 or 108 of the 1976 United States Copyright Act, without the prior written permission of the publisher.

For product information and technology assistance, contact us at

Gale Customer Support, 1-800-877-4253
For permission to use material from this text or product, submit all requests online at
www.cengage.com/permissions

Further permissions questions can be emailed to permissionrequest@cengage.com

Articles in Greenhaven Press anthologies are often edited for length to meet page requirements. In addition, original titles of these works are changed to clearly present the main thesis and to explicitly indicate the author's opinion. Every effort is made to ensure that Greenhaven Press accurately reflects the original intent of the authors. Every effort has been made to trace the owners of copyrighted material.

Cover Image copyright © Yuri Arcurs/Shutterstock.com.

LIBRARY OF CONGRESS CATALOGING-IN-PUBLICATION DATA

Netiquette and online ethics / Noah Berlatsky, book editor.
    p. cm. -- (Opposing viewpoints)
  Includes bibliographical references and index.
  ISBN 978-0-7377-6428-4 (hardcover) -- ISBN 978-0-7377-6429-1 (pbk.)
  1. Online etiquette--Juvenile literature. 2. Internet--Moral and ethical aspects--Juvenile literature. I. Berlatsky, Noah.
  TK5105.878N48 2013
  302.23'1--dc23
                                           2012043108

Printed in the United States of America
1 2 3 4 5   17 16 15 14 13

ACC LIBRARY SERVICES
AUSTIN, TX

Contents

Chapter 3: What Are the Etiquette and Ethics of Online Relationships?

Why Consider Opposing Viewpoints?

> "The only way in which a human being can make some approach to knowing the whole of a subject is by hearing what can be said about it by persons of every variety of opinion and studying all modes in which it can be looked at by every character of mind. No wise man ever acquired his wisdom in any mode but this."
>
> John Stuart Mill

In our media-intensive culture it is not difficult to find differing opinions. Thousands of newspapers and magazines and dozens of radio and television talk shows resound with differing points of view. The difficulty lies in deciding which opinion to agree with and which "experts" seem the most credible. The more inundated we become with differing opinions and claims, the more essential it is to hone critical reading and thinking skills to evaluate these ideas. Opposing Viewpoints books address this problem directly by presenting stimulating debates that can be used to enhance and teach these skills. The varied opinions contained in each book examine many different aspects of a single issue. While examining these conveniently edited opposing views, readers can develop critical thinking skills such as the ability to compare and contrast authors' credibility, facts, argumentation styles, use of persuasive techniques, and other stylistic tools. In short, the Opposing Viewpoints Series is an ideal way to attain the higher-level thinking and reading skills so essential in a culture of diverse and contradictory opinions.

In addition to providing a tool for critical thinking, Opposing Viewpoints books challenge readers to question their own strongly held opinions and assumptions. Most people form their opinions on the basis of upbringing, peer pressure, and personal, cultural, or professional bias. By reading carefully balanced opposing views, readers must directly confront new ideas as well as the opinions of those with whom they disagree. This is not to argue simplistically that everyone who reads opposing views will—or should—change his or her opinion. Instead, the series enhances readers' understanding of their own views by encouraging confrontation with opposing ideas. Careful examination of others' views can lead to the readers' understanding of the logical inconsistencies in their own opinions, perspective on why they hold an opinion, and the consideration of the possibility that their opinion requires further evaluation.

Evaluating Other Opinions

To ensure that this type of examination occurs, Opposing Viewpoints books present all types of opinions. Prominent spokespeople on different sides of each issue as well as well-known professionals from many disciplines challenge the reader. An additional goal of the series is to provide a forum for other, less known, or even unpopular viewpoints. The opinion of an ordinary person who has had to make the decision to cut off life support from a terminally ill relative, for example, may be just as valuable and provide just as much insight as a medical ethicist's professional opinion. The editors have two additional purposes in including these less known views. One, the editors encourage readers to respect others' opinions—even when not enhanced by professional credibility. It is only by reading or listening to and objectively evaluating others' ideas that one can determine whether they are worthy of consideration. Two, the inclusion of such viewpoints encourages the important critical thinking skill of objectively evaluating an author's credentials and bias. This evaluation will illuminate an author's reasons for taking a particular stance on an issue and will aid in readers' evaluation of the author's ideas.

It is our hope that these books will give readers a deeper understanding of the issues debated and an appreciation of the complexity of even seemingly simple issues when good and honest people disagree. This awareness is particularly important in a democratic society such as ours in which people enter into public debate to determine the common good. Those with whom one disagrees should not be regarded as enemies but rather as people whose views deserve careful examination and may shed light on one's own.

Thomas Jefferson once said that "difference of opinion leads to inquiry, and inquiry to truth." Jefferson, a broadly educated man, argued that "if a nation expects to be ignorant and free . . . it expects what never was and never will be." As individuals and as a nation, it is imperative that we consider the opinions of others and examine them with skill and discernment. The Opposing Viewpoints series is intended to help readers achieve this goal.

David L. Bender and Bruno Leone,
Founders

Introduction

> "There are 50 million Americans age 11
> and under. Many children are increas-
> ingly drawn to digital media, using tech-
> nology in ways many of us couldn't have
> imagined in our youth. Even for those of
> us in the media fields, it can be hard to
> keep pace with the rate at which tech-
> nology seems to evolve."
>
> —Aviva Lucas Gutnick,
> Michael Robb, Lori Takeuchi,
> and Jennifer Kotler, Always
> Connected: The New Digital Media
> Habits of Young Children, 2011

The Internet has become more and more important to people's personal and professional lives. Even children often use the Internet for entertainment and to talk to friends and family. As a result, experts and parents are trying to determine when and how children should go online, and what dangers they might face when they do connect to the web.

Children's use of the Internet is growing quickly, according to the 2011 report *Always Connected: The New Digital Media Habits of Young Children*. In 2006, the study's authors say, eight- to ten-year-olds spent an average of nineteen minutes on a computer every day. By 2009, that number had more than doubled to forty-six minutes on a computer each day. The study also found that at age three about a quarter of children go online daily; by age five, half of all children do. By age eight, more than two-thirds of children use the Internet every weekday.

Trying to regulate what age children first go online can be difficult. For instance, in a March 8, 2006, post on the *Media-*

Shift blog at PBS, Mark Glaser notes that he had originally intended to keep his son away from screens as long as he could. Instead, he writes, "Now my son is 3 and 1/2 years old and he loves typing email messages to his grandparents, and is obsessed with trying a kids' paint program on the computer."

If parents can't always enforce an age limit, however, they can often monitor or influence when and where children go online. A March 19, 2012, article on the Common Sense Media website, for example, suggests some basic safety tips. Parents, the article says, should teach kids not to share names, phone numbers, passwords, pictures, or other private information online, especially not with strangers. To avoid viruses, parents should also make sure kids know not to open e-mail or click on links from strangers. And finally, the article says, children need to be taught to go to parents if someone is bullying or harassing them online.

Many commentators also suggest that parents should monitor their children's Internet use at least to some degree. Common Sense Media recommends that parents simply put the computer in a visible and easily accessible place so adults can see which web pages children are visiting.

In an August 2, 2011, article on *MediaShift*, Dorian Benkoil discusses technological approaches to online monitoring. For example, Benkoil says that parents can control network and computer permissions so children have to ask a parent in order to download or access some materials. He also notes that in some cases parents have turned off wireless Internet connection in their homes so that computers must be accessed from specific locations.

However, Benkoil notes, such tactics do not always work. For one thing, having no wireless service may be inconvenient for parents as well as children. Furthermore, as children get older, they will become more and more adept at getting around limits on their access. Benkoil says that his own children have become experts at using proxy servers to get to restricted content. Ultimately, he suggests that it might be more useful to visit sites with children and talk to them about what they are doing there. "That way, at least, we can ask and answer questions, discuss what we're seeing and hearing, and I can gauge reactions and levels of sophistication," he says. "I'd rather have an idea of what's being consumed than believe I can place blanket restrictions."

The increasing number of children online has led to new kinds of scams and dangers. For example, in an October 10, 2011, article on CNBC, Elizabeth Alterman reports that more and more children are the victims of identity theft online. Identity thieves are especially interested in children because they have few records and because it may take years before the thieves are discovered. Children may become vulnerable if they accidentally download malware, or if a cybercriminal gets access to a computer with a child's Social Security number stored on it. A study found that 10.2 percent of children in the United States had someone else using their Social Security number, more than fifty times higher than the rate among adults.

Opposing Viewpoints: Netiquette and Online Ethics addresses these topics in chapters titled What Is the Relationship Between the Internet and Civility?, Is Cyberbullying a Serious Problem?, What Are the Etiquette and Ethics of Online Relationships?, and What Are the Etiquette and Ethics of Social Media? Throughout this volume, different authors offer varying viewpoints about how children and adults should, or should not, behave online.

CHAPTER 1

What Is the Relationship Between the Internet and Civility?

Chapter Preface

On January 8, 2011, US representative Gabrielle Giffords was shot by a gunman while greeting constituents near Tucson, Arizona. Giffords was critically injured when a bullet hit her head; six other people were killed and thirteen injured in the shooting.

The Tucson tragedy prompted a public debate about civility and animosity in politics, as well as about the Internet's role in both. In March 2010, ten months prior to the shooting, former Republican vice-presidential candidate Sarah Palin posted a map to her Facebook page in which she placed targets on a map to indicate US House seats that Republicans wanted to win in the 2010 midterm election. Giffords seat was among those targeted. In a March 24, 2010, article on the Talking Points Memo website, Jillian Rayfield reports that Palin had also written a tweet linking to the map in which she encouraged her followers by writing "Don't Retreat, Instead—RELOAD!"

Palin's comments sparked controversy at the time they were written. Critics argued that she was in effect encouraging violent attacks on the House members she had singled out. These charges became even sharper following Giffords's shooting. Arizona Democratic representative Raul Grijalva, for example, suggested a link between the shooting and the anger and incivility of the Tea Party, a right-wing movement associated with Sarah Palin. Grijalva was quoted in a January 8, 2011, *Mother Jones* article by Suzy Khimm as saying:

> [When] you stoke these flames, and you go to public meetings and you scream at the elected officials, you threaten them—you make us expendable, you make us part of the cannon fodder. For a while, you've been feeding this hatred, this division ... you feed it, you encourage it. . . . Something's going to happen. People are feeding this

monster. . . . Some of the extreme right-wing has made demonization of elected officials their priority.

Supporters of Sarah Palin, however, argued that there was no connection between the Internet map targeting Giffords's House seat and the actions of the shooter, Jared Lee Loughner. Rebecca Mansour, a Palin aide, said it was "obscene" and "appalling" to blame Palin, and added, "We never ever, ever intended it to be gun sights. It was simply crosshairs, like you'd see on maps," as quoted in a January 8, 2011, CBS News article by Brian Montopoli and Robert Hendin. Indeed, there is little evidence that Loughner was strongly associated with either the Left or the Right; his political beliefs were confused and incoherent, and he may well have been mentally ill, according to Montopoli and Hendin.

While Giffords's shooting prompted much debate on civility, there is little sign that political debate has actually become more civil following the tragedy. In a January 8, 2012, report on National Public Radio (NPR), one year after the shooting, Linton Weeks reported that Giffords was recovering, but that "incivility is easy to find on the campaign trail." Weeks added that "rudeness often dominates Internet comment sections and radio talk shows and TV town halls, leading to uncivil wars of words." Weeks acknowledged that such incivility is part of the price of free speech and democratic debate. But at the same time, the shooting in Tucson suggests that politicians and the public need to be careful that incivility does not become so extreme that it leads to violence and tragedy.

In the following chapter, different authors debate the relationship between the Internet and incivility, as well as the use of incivility within democratic debate.

> "We are a loud and messy bunch, but, in many ways, we're much more civil than our forebears."

Incivility in Our Society Has Not Increased

Kathleen Cairns

Kathleen Cairns teaches women's history at California Polytechnic State University and is the author of The Enigma Woman: The Death Penalty of Nellie May Madison. *In the following viewpoint, she argues that our society is more civil than it used to be. She points out that in the past, people used racial slurs and committed public lynching. She also argues that women were treated with contempt as well as subjected to verbal and sometimes physical abuse, and that gay people faced even more prejudice than they do today. Racism, sexism, and homophobia are less tolerated today, Cairns says, which she concludes is evidence of an increase, not a decrease, in civility.*

As you read, consider the following questions:

1. What does Cairns say is the difference between American incivility in the past and incivility today?

Kathleen Cairns, "Viewpoint: Incivility Not New," SanLuisObispo.com, March 29, 2012. Copyright © 2012 by Kathleen Cairns. All rights reserved. Reproduced by permission.

2. How was child abuse treated differently in the past than it is today, according to Cairns?

3. What was the Emmett Till murder, and how does Cairns say it would be treated differently today than in the past?

[Syndicated columnist] Kathleen Parker's March 26 [2012] column focused on a topic that seems to be in the forefront of public debate these days—the lack of civility, both in politics and in daily life. It's hard not to agree wholeheartedly, when every day we're subjected to shouting politicians, bombastic (and misogynistic) talk radio hosts, yakking cell phone users and distracted drivers texting and listening to thumping music at the same time (how do they do it?).

Racism as Incivility

But disagree I must. If we're talking about how people behave in public—the clothes they wear (or don't), the language they use (@#$#@), their stubborn insistence that the world see (and, apparently, comment on) every facet of their lives; well, yes, modern life surely seems "uncivil."

Blame it on the media; in fact, blame everything on the media—reality TV shows, talk radio, confessional TV programs, blogs, various forms of social media that make it easy to show the world who we are and exactly what we think, 24/7. It all started, arguably, in June 1994, with that slo-mo [slow-motion] car "chase" down an L.A. freeway; the white Bronco ferrying O.J. Simpson somewhere, police and TV cameras in pursuit.[1] Now we can't seem to get enough of this stuff. It's like a pileup that everyone slows down to watch.

But incivility has always existed in American society. The difference is that it mostly, but not always, occurred behind closed doors, or under cover of authority of one sort or an-

1. O.J. Simpson was a famous football player. He was accused of murdering his wife and her friend. He was acquitted of the murders in a massively publicized trial.

other. Lynching took place outside, and it surely was much worse than uncivil. Even many participants seemed to realize this, since they took great care to wear hoods or sheets to avoid recognition. Lynching was not "legal," per se, but those in authority looked the other way. In the few cases where perpetrators were prosecuted, white juries quickly acquitted the defendants and welcomed them back into the community.

Racial epithets can surely be considered "uncivil," and yet, in many parts of the country—in fact, in my own family—whites used to drop them casually into daily conversations, never considering, or caring, that they might be hurtful or demeaning. Epithets went along with restrictive covenants and sunset laws, designed to keep people of color out of white neighborhoods, except for daylight hours when they cooked, cleaned and mowed the lawns.

Greater Civility Today

But the incivility didn't start and end with "race." Female rape victims who dared to confront their perpetrators in court faced a judicial system that seemed to place them on trial. What were they wearing? Had they ever had sex with anyone besides their husbands? And why were they in that dangerous place? Didn't they know what would happen? Husbands could force sex upon their wives without having it called "rape" until the late 1970s. Uncivil, you bet; ditto for crude sexual remarks and gestures that were part of the cultural and social argot. Watch *Mad Men* [a television show about an advertising firm in the 1960s] if you want to see (and hopefully wince at) sexual attitudes and behavior from the "good old days."

I could go on and on; about child abuse—both sexual and physical—for example. Children came to school battered, bruised and traumatized. Teachers and others were strongly encouraged to look the other way; after all, families were sacred, private entities. Hear no evil, see no evil. Gay men and women stayed carefully in the closet, unless they knew what

Selective Incivility as Discrimination

While conceptually distinct, incivility, gender harassment, and racial harassment have common qualities: degradation, intimidation, or offense of the target, as well as violation of social norms dictating that workplace relations be respectful. [Lilia M.] Cortina (2008) has proposed that these behaviors are, at times, one and the same. This may seem implausible, with "generally" uncivil conduct making no overt reference to gender, race, or other social category. However, when women and people of color are selectively targeted, incivility may represent a *covert* manifestation of gender or race bias. Cortina has dubbed this phenomenon *selective incivility*, conceptualizing it as a place where sexism, racism, and incivility collide. . . .

Cortina (2008) specifically proposed that, in many organizations, women and people of color encounter more uncivil treatment than men and whites. With incivility being subtle (e.g., being ignored, interrupted, or excluded from professional camaraderie) and ambiguous with respect to intent (e.g., accompanied by apologies. "I didn't see you." "I'm exhausted"), it often escapes the attention of management. On its surface, the behavior is also neutral with respect to gender and race, which makes it challenging to bring about accusations of Title VII violation [that is, civil rights violations]. Cortina (ibid.) thus argued that incivility provides a means by which individuals can discriminate (even unintentionally and unconsciously) against women and people of color, while preserving an image of themselves as egalitarian.

Suzy Fox and Terri R. Lituchy, eds.
Gender and the Dysfunctional Workplace. *Cheltenham, UK: Edward Edgar Publishing, 2012, pp. 109–110.*

was good for them. My uncle learned that lesson the hard way, when he "came out" to his family in the 1950s and was quickly and quietly disowned. Wait, that still happens.

Would I prefer to live in a society where people didn't revel in showing their worst sides to the world at large, where teenage boys wore pants that covered their private parts and where I didn't have to quickly change radio and TV channels at the first sound of the grating voices of certain, unnamed "personalities"? Of course. Would I ever go back to the good old days? Never; we are a loud and messy bunch, but, in many ways, we're much more civil than our forebears.

In the summer of 1955, 14-year-old Emmett Till went South from Chicago to visit a relative in Mississippi. He reportedly engaged in conversation with a white woman and, shortly afterward, was kidnapped, beaten, shot to death and dumped in the Tallahatchie River. The killing mobilized the African-American community; thousands attended his funeral. Two men were brought to trial and acquitted, despite widespread recognition of their guilt. Today, Till is viewed as a catalyst for the civil rights movement, but at the time, few white people commented on, or cared about, the murder. If the Till murder had occurred today, the story would have gone viral within hours and Americans of all ethnicities would have added their voices to the chorus demanding justice. That is what a "civil" society does.

> *"Mostly, comment forums remind me of children's playgrounds, where the bullies always win—because everyone else scarpers."*

Online Incivility Coarsens Public Discourse

Andrew Stafford

Andrew Stafford is an Australian author and a contributor to the Age. *In the following viewpoint, he reports on a small publication that has disabled comments on its website. He argues that comments sections tend to be abusive and misogynist, and that they are often the target of "trolls"—individuals who harass others online—and "astroturfers"—people online concealing that they are paid advocates for a particular position. He argues that comments should be much better policed and anonymity should be banned. The alternative, he says, is an ongoing coarsening of public discussion.*

As you read, consider the following questions:

1. According to the author, what is the *King's Tribune*, and what is its circulation?

Andrew Stafford, "Who Are These Haters That Poison the Well of Our Discourse?," *Sydney Morning Herald*, April 12, 2012. Copyright © 2012 by Andrew Stafford. All rights reserved. Reproduced by permission.

2. Under what conditions does Stafford say that anonymity might be reasonable for individuals who place comments?

3. What are Stafford's three wishes for comments sections?

In the online edition of Melbourne-based publication the *King's Tribune* last month [March 2012], editors Jane and Justin Shaw came to a radical decision. They resolved—after a few months of earnest consideration was capped by one post of anonymous, misogynist bilge too many—to turn comments on their website "off".

Disabling Comments

Given the magazine deals mostly in robustly expressed opinion, and not wishing to discourage debate, the Shaws made an even more radical suggestion: letters could be sent by e-mail or Facebook, or even (are you sitting down?) by post. The most cogent, topical and witty of them would be considered for publication.

It's important to note the *Tribune* is a small venture. It began five years ago as a newsletter for a St Kilda bar and became a "real" magazine last October, extending its reach through newsagents into Sydney and Canberra. Its circulation is less than 1000; the Shaws keep day jobs.

There are practical reasons for a small publication like the *Tribune* to disable comments: neither the editors nor individual writers have the time, energy or inclination to monitor and moderate, much less reply to them all. There are more pressing things, such as getting out the next issue.

The *Tribune* is not alone. Many bloggers are heading down the same path, which seems counterintuitive, given immediacy and interactivity were two of the key attractions of blogging in the first place. But how many people are actually bothering to read the so-called bottom half of the Internet, let alone add to it?

My guess is that it's a tiny minority, but it's a minority that's having a disproportionate influence on both the tone and direction of the print and electronic media.

The key question for older mastheads in particular is how much immediate, non-considered, anonymous commentary enhances public debate—after they've spent valuable resources weeding out the spammers, trollers, and astroturfers[1] that deliberately seek to distort and/or poison it.

There's some evidence the astroturfers, in particular, are on the march. British writer George Monbiot recently told of being contacted by a whistleblower that worked as part of a PR [public relations] team paid to infiltrate comment threads and forums, doing the bidding of their corporate clients. The whistleblower worked under 70 different usernames.

The implications for debates on contentious topics such as climate change—which is not actually scientifically contentious, unless you have an enormous vested interest in convincing the public otherwise, or at least sowing the seeds of confusion and doubt—are obvious. And alarming.

Then there's the issue of anonymity. This might be vital if you're a Chinese or Syrian dissident or, for that matter, a spambot turned corporate whistleblower. Mostly, though, it just allows people to indulge their worst tendencies, not only towards individuals but entire social groups.

In this respect, a culture of widespread online bullying—particularly towards female writers—actually has the potential to drive some of our brightest voices out of public life altogether. Writers have always needed thick hides, but for some the price of your anonymity can be measured in their therapy bills.

It's true that people haven't changed in their tendency to be biased, ill-informed, unreasonable or at times plain inar-

---

1. Spammers place advertising links in comments. Trolls deliberately post inflammatory comments. Astroturfers pose as anonymous individuals who are placing comments but are actually being paid to express a particular view.

"The anonymous commenter in action," cartoon by Wilfred Hildonen, www.Cartoon Stock.com.

ticulate, and that we shouldn't blame the technology (which can also be such a transformative agent for good) for the shortcomings of those who abuse it.

Controversy Defeats Reason

After all, people can also be wise, considerate, challenging and eminently reasonable, and they too can reach a wider audience than ever before. In practice, though, this rarely happens. Mostly, comment forums remind me of children's playgrounds, where the bullies always win—because everyone else scarpers.

The sad truth is that controversy outrates reason every time. We live in an immoderate age. It's why Ray Hadley, Kyle Sandilands, Alan Jones and Andrew Bolt [all Australian media personalities] are among the best-paid and most powerful media personalities in the country.

Does the popularity of *The Drum, The Punch* and even, for that matter, *Q&A* [Australian news shows] depend first and foremost on the talent of their writers and guests? Or do they live or die on the extent of the frenzy they generate? This is a difficult dilemma for mainstream media publications, which (unlike the *King's Tribune*) base part of their online business models on advertising page views.

The genie is long out of the bottle, to the point that it's both impossible and undesirable to stuff it back in. But, were the genie able to grant three wishes, I'd request genuine transparency of identity (why can't names and addresses be withheld, where clearly necessary, on request?), a much tougher line on personal abuse and a greater weighting towards comments that actually expand discussion.

All of which takes time, money and human resources. But with the nation's political and personal manners [growing] increasingly coarse, it might help elevate the tone of how we speak to each other, and provide at least some protection from an army of baiters, haters and spivs [slackers].

> "*The Internet has changed all that. There is now a new public sphere and many more people have access to it, and they are using it to say what they could only grumble about in private.*"

Online Incivility Is Part of Greater Democratic Participation and Changing Norms

Mano Singham

Mano Singham is a theoretical physicist and the author of Quest for Truth: Scientific Progress and Religious Belief. *In the following viewpoint, he argues that the Internet has created new norms for public civility. In the past, he says, there were only a few people able to gain a public platform, and in order to talk to such people, others were required to be polite. However, he says, the Internet has opened the public sphere to all. As a result, he says, those who speak in public face harsh criticism and are held much more accountable. He concludes that the public sphere is better for it.*

Mano Singham, "On Insults-2: Heated Language on the Internet," Freethoughtblogs.com, March 15, 2012. Copyright © 2012 by Mano Singham. All rights reserved. Reproduced by permission.

As you read, consider the following questions:

1. Of what uncivil behavior does Singham say he has been personally accused?

2. Under what circumstances does Singham say that people were scathing in their criticisms of public figures before the Internet?

3. What does Singham identify as Rush Limbaugh's transgression, and what was the result of it?

Once in a while, a furious debate flares up about the proper tone that people should use in exchanges with one another on the Internet. This occurs within the skeptic community as well, the most prominent division being between the groups now referred to as accommodationists and the new atheists. The most common charge laid against the latter is that they sometimes use intemperate language in criticizing both religion and the accommodationist position.[1]

New Norms

I too have been occasionally accused of displaying a sense of superiority and cynicism, and ridiculing and making fun of people who disagree with me. There is some justification for this latter charge but the fact that people think it is something that should be complained about arises from two factors: (1) people not being aware that the norms in the new public sphere created by the Internet are quite different from that of the old public sphere; and (2) conflating the norms of the private sphere with those of the old and new public sphere.

Before the dawn of the Internet, there was tight control of who had access to the public sphere. It was only the media organizations and a select few nonthreatening public intellectu-

---

1. "New atheists" is the name given to a group of twenty-first-century atheist writers who believe religion should be refuted and criticized, not just tolerated. Accommodationists take a less confrontational atheist position.

als who could get their views disseminated widely. There was little recourse for any member of the general public to get their point of view heard, even if news reports or the commentators were flat out wrong about the facts. All one could do was write a letter to the editor of the publication or the author of the piece and hope that they would deign to respond. To get even an acknowledgment that they had heard you was rare and to get a correction was even rarer.

This completely unequal power relationship resulted in the public having to take a supplicatory attitude when approaching these powerful people who had access to the public space, hoping that by being obsequious one could get one's foot in the door. It also resulted in a sense of arrogance on the part of those who had access to the public sphere, who were easily seduced into thinking they had superior intellect and judgment simply because they were rarely challenged. And they became used to being treated deferentially.

Of course, ordinary people could be quite scathing in their criticisms of what they read and heard but these views could only be expressed in private to their immediate circle and rarely entered the public debate. So journalists and commentators and public intellectuals could say what they wanted. As long as news editors and their bosses did not mind, they were free from challenge.

The Internet has changed all that. There is now a new public sphere and many more people have access to it, and they are using it to say what they could only grumble about in private, and I suspect that they are expressing it in the same strong way they used to do before. Now the words of politicians, journalists, and others are subjected to close scrutiny and there is immediate public push back when they get something wrong. Many simply have not adjusted to the fact that they no longer occupy Mount Olympus, out of reach of the rabble. And they definitely are not used to the fact that the scathing criticisms that earlier could only be voiced in private (and which they could ignore even in the unlikely event that they heard them at all) are now being given much wider airing. It is such people who often complain about the 'lack of civility' in the modern media era. What they do not seem to realize is that this 'lack of civility' always existed but it just did not reach their ears.

Immediate Push Back

It is a different world now. I can point to numerous examples where public figures have been taken to task *immediately* by a chorus of criticisms about things they got wrong and have been forced to correct and backtrack. It is no longer possible for them to use ignorance as an excuse to continue to repeat falsehoods or discredited ideas. The immediate firestorm that erupted around Rush Limbaugh's comments about Sandra Fluke and forced him to make an apology was enabled by the Internet. His transgression was that he personalized a political issue, and tried to discredit the position Fluke was taking by attacking her as a person.[2] In an earlier age, he would have got away with it. But in the Internet age, you have to expect to receive in kind whatever you dish out. Limbaugh's single big megaphone is now counterbalanced by many people with small megaphones.

Were some of Limbaugh's critics also intemperate in their language? Very likely. But that is the nature of the Internet, where the public actions and words of people are subject to any and all manner of criticisms, and what was once articulated only to those in the immediate vicinity are now available to the whole world. This is the new reality, and while there are those who find it distasteful, there is nothing they can do about it or, in my opinion, should be able to do about it. They have to learn to live with vigorous and robust (and

---

2. Sandra Fluke was a Georgetown University law student invited by House Democrats to speak before Congress. After she did so, Rush Limbaugh, a radio talk show host, made inflammatory comments about her on his talk show.

sometimes rude, crude, and profane) public speech. This does not mean they have to conform. Each person can choose how he or she wishes to behave in this new public sphere and can choose what they want to read or see or listen to. But it is futile to complain about the rhetorical style of others on the Internet.

Having said all that, I have to emphasize something I have stressed repeatedly, that the norms in the private sphere have not changed that much. When one is talking to people directly, face-to-face in a private setting, a completely different and more traditional set of norms still apply. Civility still largely rules. But people should not expect those norms to be observed in public settings.

The Internet kitchen is hot. If you can't stand it, you shouldn't enter.

| *"The data ... show that citizens use comment boards to vent and bloviate."*

Online Incivility Exists, but Its Effects Are Difficult to Determine

Robert M. Eisinger

Robert M. Eisinger is the dean of the School of Liberal Arts at the Savannah College of Art and Design. In the following viewpoint, he reports on his project of cataloging instances of incivility in political comment threads online. He reports that there are many instances of incivility in such comment threads, even in cases where moderators claim to be screening for incivility. However, he says that incivility has long been an aspect of democracy. He concludes that it is difficult to determine the effect of incivility on democracy.

As you read, consider the following questions:

1. What are two reasons the *New York Times* says that it will censor or remove comments?

2. According to Eisinger, of the 350 comments sampled from the *New York Times* how many contained obscene language?

Robert M. Eisinger, "Incivility on the Internet: Dilemmas for Democratic Discourse," Revised version of *APSA 2011 Annual Meeting Paper*, 2011, pp. 1–23. Copyright © 2011 by Robert M. Eisinger. All rights reserved. Reproduced by permission.

3. How does democracy benefit from incivility, according to Michael Schudson?

Whether the Internet is good or bad for democracy is a question too simple to ask and too broad to answer—even more so given the nascent body of literature on the topic. Rather a more manageable puzzle worthy of analysis concerns the tone of Internet discourse, and whether the sometimes cacophonous voices heard in the blogosphere are as contentious as frequently described in popular media. Examples abound of Internet conversations that veer into or are in the midst of vitriol. But are those expressions of uncivil thoughts and opinions representative of or exceptions to Internet discourse? As more media publications provide outlets for citizens to respond to the news, most notably in the form of comment boards following an article, questions arise about the qualitative tone of those comments. What does Internet discourse on comment boards sound and look like? What impact might it have on democratic rule? ...

Measuring Incivility

Devising a method for measuring the incivility on Internet comment boards is challenging, elusive and arguably subjective. . . .

Borrowing from [Sarah] Sobieraj and [Jeffrey M.] Barry's 2011 work, I initially used seven variables that capture incivility. These variables are: (a) insulting language, (b) name-calling, (c) verbal fighting/sparring, (d) character assassination, (e) conflagration, (f) belittling, and (g) obscene language. . . . But some of these variables were subject to interpretation by coders and so these variables did not prove reliable. I then narrowed the analysis to two of these variables—character assassination and obscene language. These two variables are among the more extreme manifestations of incivility, less subjective to identify, and more likely to capture uncivil comments when they are present.

Seventeen articles from popularly read news and political websites were read and coded. Popularity was determined using eBizMBA, which tracks web traffic. Six websites, all in the top 15 for June 2011, were chosen. Listed alphabetically, they were CNN, *Huffington Post*, Politico, the *New York Times*, *Washington Post*, and Yahoo! News. For each media source, two articles were chosen and coded from the week of June 13–20, 2011, and from January 1–26, 2012. In each case, either the most popular web article from that day (as determined by the news source), or the article with the most comments (also determined by the news source) [was coded]. When popularity and most-commented article were not provided, the lead story was coded, determined by the cover story article with the largest font headline. These determinations are not easy to locate, as 'popularity' and 'most frequently read' evolves as the day transpires. I therefore chose each article in the late afternoon or evening, attempting to assure that there was a sufficient measure of readership from the U.S. West Coast for each popularly commented story being coded. It should also be noted that news organizations now employ moderators and web editors who are instructed to filter comments they deem unacceptable or offensive. The presence of these editors and moderators would suggest that Internet incivility may be tempered or attenuated in these results.

Coding was performed independently by two persons. Each was given specific instructions, directions and guidelines about how to identify incivility. Each was tasked to read the first 150 comments, and identify if the comments included either obscenity or character assassination. Internet comments sometimes exceed thousands per article; the 150 limit was chosen to ensure that a sufficient number of comments were coded in a timely manner. Comments were coded in the order they were made. That is, the first coded comment was the first comment made following the article, as compared to the most recently typed commentary. In total, 2552 comments were coded. Overall percent agreement by the two coders was 89% for character assassination (Scott's Pi 0.407), and 98% for obscenity (Scott's Pi 0.583). Topics ranged from [Republican presidential candidate] Mitt Romney's debate performance, the Federal Bureau of Investigation (FBI) and privacy rights, President [Barack] Obama's fund-raising strategy, Federal Reserve chairman Ben Bernanke's views on the debt ceiling, Pakistan's arresting of Central Intelligence Agency (CIA) informants, the life expectancy of U.S. citizens, Congressman Anthony Weiner's resignation [following a scandal involving lewd text messages], the murder trial of Casey Anthony [on trial for the murder of her two-year-old daughter, Caylee], political unrest in Syria, riots in Vancouver after the Stanley Cup [hockey] final game, executive pay, and a comedy impersonator of President Obama.

Degrees of Incivility

The comments following the [seventeen] articles coded reveal significant amounts of incivility.... Because comments from only seventeen articles from six media outlets were coded, it would be unwise to draw any conclusions about comparing those media outlets. Similarly, while there was a range of topics discussed in each article, [seventeen] articles are too few to generate hypotheses about incivility by topic. A few key findings are worth highlighting:

- Uncivil discourse, when narrowly defined by obscenity and character assassination, occurs in all of the coded articles.

- Comments are avoiding the moderators "filtering" of uncivil comments.

The *New York Times* moderates its online reader comments. One *New York Times* employee familiar with the process notes the guidelines:

Guidelines on moderation establish that comments are to be rejected when they are uncivil or include ad hominem attacks, either on other readers or the writer of a piece; profanity or obscenity; promotion of something off-topic; or incoherent statements.

This point is underscored in a 2007 *Times* document, titled "The Top 10 Reasons We Deleted Your Comment." The first two points read as follows:

1. You called someone an idiot, a moron, a dope, a dummy, or something else uncivil. No name-calling and personal abuse, please.

2. You used profanity. Our rules forbid even mild oaths and vulgarities that are now common on TV and the web. We know people talk this way every day, even in our newsroom, but certain words do still offend and anger people, or at the very least make them less likely to come back here. If you wouldn't say it in front of your mother, a minister or a 5-year-old, think twice about saying it here. That includes masked or veiled profanities that combine letters and dashes. Don't even call the word to mind.

Our data show that overall, the second rule is being enforced. Of the 350 comments sampled from the *Times*, only two contained obscene language. However in the initial analysis of seven uncivil variables, it was discovered that belittling, name-calling and conflagrating comments proliferate, not only in the *Times'* comments, but in the other five websites investigated. "[E]vil fat cats," "Wall Street's errand boy," "hypocrite," and "pathetic" are a few of the terms used to describe individuals in one *Times* article. Other terms (e.g., "Community organizing = choreographed shakedown," "now the entire White House is used to trade policy for political payola," "President Obama and the democratic power brokers in DC you can kiss my you know what") are more dubious. The overarching point here is that while obscenity is rare/ nonexistent (in *Times* comments), it sometimes finds its way into the comment discourse. Some forms of incivility, like obscenity, elude censors by the use of clever typing, while other forms are more subjective and do not raise any immediate red flags among discussion moderators.

Forms of Incivility

- Incivility is difficult to measure. Both coders noted how belittling and conflagration, for example, are subjective and difficult to code. This is less true of obscenity or character assassination. Inter-coder reliability was higher when limited to these two variables (0.407 and 0.583), compared to coding the seven variables (Scott's Pi maximum of 0.19), for verbal sparring. What appears to be sarcasm to one coder may be inflaming, conflagrating verbal sparring to another, or alternatively, humorous banter.

- Second, the comments are not easily or naturally read in an isolated phrase or even sentence. Incivility may transcend categories, suggesting that comments are read and coded holistically, not in parts or parcels. As such, the civility (or lack thereof) is based both on a strict interpretation of the coding categories, and by a holistic, complete reading of the same commentary. This last point suggests that while coding of incivility may be subjective (that is, what is inflaming to one coder may not always be inflaming to another), there is ample [evidence] that incivility is often layered and contextual.

- Additionally, the comments are often personalized. Rather than engaging in a dialogue, some citizens start arguments with a mean-spiritedness. While one can

Number of Uncivil Comments in 150 Comments

Article	Number of Uncivil Comments	%
Casey Anthony, CNN	Coder A = 9	6.0
	Coder B = 30	20.0
Ben Bernanke, CNN	Coder A = 36	24.0
	Coder B = 34	22.7
Vancouver Riots, *Huffington Post*	Coder A = 5	3.3
	Coder B = 11	7.3
Syrian Troops, *Huffington Post*	Coder A = 5	3.3
	Coder B =12	8.0
President Obama and Wall Street, *New York Times*	Coder A = 32	21.3
	Coder B = 36	24.0
FBI Privacy, *New York Times*	Coder A = 46	30.7
	Coder B = 24	16.0
Mitt Romney, Politico	Coder A = 73	48.7
	Coder B = 44	29.3
Obama Impersonator, Politico	Coder A = 43	28.6
	Coder B = 64	42.7
Executive Pay, *Washington Post*	Coder A = 10	6.6
	Coder B = 19	12.7
Life Expectancy, *Washington Post*	Coder A = 27	18.0
	Coder B = 37	24.7
Weiner Resignation, Yahoo	Coder A = 31	20.7
	Coder B = 44	29.3
Pakistan/CIA, Yahoo	Coder A = 24	16.0
	Coder B = 35	23.3

TAKEN FROM: Robert Eisinger, "Incivility on the Internet: Dilemmas for Democratic Discourse," *APSA 2011 Annual Meeting Paper*, p. 12.

argue that incivility is at times subjective, there are numerous examples of extreme incivility, suggesting that, at times, deliberative discourse is nonexistent. The following examples exemplify the more intense forms of incivility discovered: . . .

Thus the real beliefs of Muslims. This shows that most Muslims believe in hatred, intolerance, and oppression through violence. And that the unbelievers will pay. People like you don't belong in civilization. Muslims are like two-year-old children who only can see what they want and not see they are a small unimportant organization that must kill people in order to garner attention. Kathy, Yahoo!/Reuters, "Pakistan Arrests CIA's bin Laden Informants: Report," June 15, 2011

Can't we put this j-rkoff in a helicopter and drop him over the pacific? BanThis1Too, CNNMoney, "Bernanke: Stop Holding Debt Ceiling Hostage," June 14, 2011

Pls kill yourself as soon as possible. Your country is a piece of evil s---!!! John, Yahoo!/Reuters, "Pakistan Arrests CIA's bin Laden Informants: Report," June 15, 2011

This guy should be dangling from a rope, not advising our president. He wants to raise the debt ceiling so he can funnel more stolen money back to his "Bank of London" masters. Christopher Lusk, CNNMoney, "Bernanke: Stop Holding Debt Ceiling Hostage," June 14, 2011

Generally I'm pro-life, but I wish you had been aborted. We need less morons like yourself reproducing. Hopefully you'll relegate your great wisdom to the comments section of CNN. jm999 CNN.com, "Casey Anthony's Trial Is a Summer Obsession," June 16, 2011

Oh, shut up! Congress won't act, so he is taking his case to the people. Popular support will force Congress to do the right thing for the country and if not, they can go home! Notice the Debt Ceiling remark? What that cost us? it sure did! For no other reason but to be big a$$es! They lose!

That was the guy I voted for. Patriot265, *Washington Post*, "State of the Union 2012: Obama Speech Transcipt," January 24, 2012

You very well may be the biggest dummy on this blog. Slap yourself dude. Btwixdalines, CNN, "Iran Warns U.S. over Aircraft Carrier," January 3, 2012

Each of these comments is a screed, but not all of them contain obscenity or character assassination. The comments sometimes digress from the topic of the news article to a dialogue between citizens. For example, an article about Pakistan becomes a means through which citizens complain about the Obama administration, or Congressman Anthony Weiner's resignation is an excuse to besmirch Democrats. Regardless of topic, the article becomes an excuse to write a missive.

Incivility Now and in the Past

The research collected here indicates a prevalence of online political talk that is at times uncivil. Of the 2552 comments, approximately 2% are obscene and 5% are character assassinating.

How does one interpret these findings? At first glance, they do not bode well for those who believe that civil discourse, even through the Internet, enhances democracy. Incivility exists, about many topics and on many websites. Even with the web editors and comment board moderators, one finds obscenity and gratuitous attacks on individuals, both public officials and citizens (strangers) who disagree with a particular posting. As [Kevin A.] Hill and [John E.] Hughes note, "[c]hat rooms are a difficult format for thoughtful discussion. The short line space and the fast pace require people to make snap comments, not thoughtful ones." The data here show that citizens use comment boards to vent and bloviate, and often do so in a tone that by anyone's standards cannot be considered polite, thoughtful, capacious or welcoming.

That written, incivility has been with us forever. While comment boards have been popularized, one need not equate the uncivil comments with the demise of the republic or the media industry. The mere existence of incivility is noteworthy, but incivility by itself may not stifle discourse. In some cases, uncivil commentary can enhance deliberative conversation. [Michael] Schudson reminds us that democratic talk requires a "degree of sociability or, at least, civility" but that democracy is also "deeply uncomfortable." He writes:

> [D]emocracy may require withdrawal from civility itself. Democracy may sometimes require that your interlocutor does not wait politely for you to finish but shakes you by the collar and cries "Listen! Listen for God's sake!". . . We call the people who initiate such departures from civility driven, ambitious, unreasonable, self-serving, rude, hot-headed, self-absorbed—the likes of Newt Gingrich [a conservative Speaker of the House of Representatives in the 1990s] and Martin Luther King Jr. [1960s civil rights leader] and William Lloyd Garrison [an abolitionist before the Civil War]. All of these are people willing to engage in democratic conversation but also pugnacious beyond the point of civility. . . .

In short, there is ample room for some incivility within democracy. How much, where, when and by whom remain questions worth debating. In addition to the possible positive effects of absorbing contested points of view (e.g., active processing of and reconsideration of one's own views, possible increased interest in voting), it is worth remembering the findings of [Deborah Jordan] Brooks and [John G.] Geer, who note that, "The American public is quite resilient to the nasty exchanges now prevalent in U.S. political discourse.". . .

It appears however that the democratization of public opinion has also brought with it the coarsening of public expression. Deliberation requires contemplation beyond mean-spirited missives. The findings in this [viewpoint] suggest at minimum recurring nastiness and personal malice aimed at and among fellow engaged citizens. Citizens who do not know one another engage in obscenity-infused vitriol, as they appear to amuse themselves belittling and sparring with virtual-digital enemies. Some commenters develop a virtual reputation, with their comments greeted by others in the forum with a 'here we go again' mentality. . . . Here one must be careful not to argue that only refined civil discourse is welcomed, or that all vulgar, boorish dialogue must be filtered or censored. Rather, incivility is neither a toggle switch nor a dichotomous variable, and its effects are not straightforward. It is at times subjective and has shades of intensity. Incivility may provoke some to opine, while silencing others. Political theorists and communication scholars should advance these discussions about the tone of citizen discourse precisely because such comments are textured, complex, and rife with multiple interpretations.

But these comments are not written or read accidentally. Rather than misidentify them with a particular or narrow definition (e.g., soft, hard, news, entertainment), they are in fact a unique combination of fact, opinion and entertainment. . . . Some citizens, arguably many more than the data reveal here, are reading and writing about politics in an uncivil tone that should engage if not concern democratic theorists, communication and public opinion scholars, public officials and all interested citizens seeking to encourage civic engagement.

| *"The root of harassment lies with ano-nymity."*

Online Anonymity Encourages Harassment of Women

Allison McNeely

Allison McNeely is a writer and editor and the cohost of Calgary's feminist radio program Yeah, What She Said. *In the following viewpoint, she argues that anonymity enables and encourages online abuse. She says that women and feminists are especially likely to be the targets of this abuse because of misogyny. She argues that Canada should pass new laws targeting online abusers, and she encourages women to continue writing and speaking out despite the vicious attacks they may encounter online.*

As you read, consider the following questions:

1. According to McNeely, why do people attack feminist blogs and feminists?

2. Under Canadian civil law, why could someone be found guilty of defamation, according to McNeely?

3. What does Jennie Palmer say is the risk for her writing online?

Allison McNeely, "Internet 'Rife' with Harassment for Feminists," *Calgary Journal*, November 7, 2011. Copyright © 2011 by Allison McNeely. All rights reserved. Reproduced by permission.

Depending on whom you ask, the Internet is an open source haven for sharing, learning and communicating, or it's a place rife with hate and intimidation. The virtue of the Internet—its deregulation—has allowed us to harass and stalk each other without consequence. It's the "Digital Wild West."

Attacks Online Are Easy

Feminist blogs are a target for hate on the Internet. Why people attack feminist blogs is the same as why people attack feminists in real life: They question and criticize traditional ideas about gender and sexuality in our society. That's threatening. People attack when they feel threatened and it's a lot easier to attack someone online than it is to do in person.

The root of harassment lies with anonymity. If you create a username and learn how to mask your IP [Internet protocol] address, it can [be] very difficult for the average Internet user to determine the true identity of the troll [referring to someone who harasses others online] who is attacking them.

Furthermore, there is no specific section of Canadian law that deals with online harassment.

The Canadian criminal code deals with cyberbullying as harassment or defamatory libel, in which a statement is directed against someone that could seriously hurt their reputation.

Under Canadian civil law, someone could be found guilty of defamation, creating an unsafe environment or be held responsible for actions that they could have foreseen happening, such as someone killing themselves as a result of online bullying.

Online harassment often goes unnoticed and unpunished, and feminist bloggers, as well as other Internet users, are left to decide how to conduct themselves and how to respond to hateful comments online.

A Tough Place for Women

Jennie Palmer, a cohost of *Yeah, What She Said* on CJSW 90.9 FM and a feminist blogger, has experienced her share of online harassment.

Palmer wrote a blog post about popular sexist and offensive "de-motivational posters" that she received in an e-mail. She received hateful comments on her blog. . . .

Palmer chooses to leave negative comments on her blog and she advises feminist bloggers to be prepared.

"Do your research and write respectfully, but don't be afraid to be opinionated. Bloggers who let their personality and opinion shine through have the most interesting posts."

Palmer acknowledges that there is a certain risk with writing online—namely that coworkers or strangers may think she is "crazy" because of her blog. As a feminist blogger, I've shared her fears.

The Internet is a tough place for women, no matter what they do. A 2006 study at the University of Maryland found that users with a female pseudonym are 25 times more likely to be harassed online than users with male or ambiguous pseudonyms.

It seems that the solution to cyberbullying is what Palmer is doing—do your research, keep writing, screw the haters.

But it can't continue this way forever. The problem of online bullying and harassment is not unique to feminists. Gay teenagers are killing themselves because of unpunished harassment.

There should be provisions that deal specifically with online harassment in our civil and criminal law. It should not come down to defamation or libel, because that can be extremely hard to prove in court.

We need to publish harassing comments. Whether one responds to them or not is a personal choice, but refusing to let harassment make you feel ashamed is a start.

Finally, we need to lose the idea that someone is "asking for it." Just because you share your opinion online does not mean that you deserve to be abused. Hate is hate, even in the Wild West.

"'Real names' policies aren't empower-ing; they're an authoritarian assertion of power over vulnerable people."

Online Anonymity Protects Marginalized Groups

danah boyd

danah boyd is a senior researcher at Microsoft Research and a research assistant professor in media, culture, and communica-tion at New York University. In the following viewpoint, she ar-gues that real-name policies that prevent people from being anonymous online hurt the disadvantaged and marginalized. She argues that women and minorities are often the targets of harassment online. Using pseudonyms, she says, can provide a level of protection and make it possible for the disempowered to speak. She concludes that real-name policies do not protect users but instead put them at risk, and are therefore an abuse of power.

As you read, consider the following questions:

1. What are three reasons for anonymity given by Kirrily "Skud" Robert's survey participants?

danah boyd, "'Real Names' Policies Are an Abuse of Power," *Apophenia*, August 4, 2011. http://www.zephoria.org. Copyright © 2011 by danah boyd. All rights reserved. Repro-duced by permission.

2. What was Google Plus's mistake that prevented it from dictating a "real names" policy, and why does the author say it was a mistake?

3. What example does the author use to show that the issue of reputation and real names online must be altered when discussing marginalized people?

Everyone's abuzz with the "nymwars," mostly in response to Google Plus's [an online social network] decision to enforce its "real names" policy. At first, Google Plus went on a deleting spree, killing off accounts that violated its policy. When the community reacted with outrage, Google Plus leaders tried to calm the anger by detailing their "new and improved" mechanism to enforce "real names" (without killing off accounts). This only sparked increased discussion about the value of pseudonymity. Dozens of blog posts have popped up with people expressing their support for pseudonymity and explaining their reasons.

Reasons for Anonymity

One of the posts, by Kirrily "Skud" Robert included a list of explanations that came from people she polled, including:

- "I am a high school teacher, privacy is of the utmost importance."

- "I have used this name/account in a work context, my entire family know this name and my friends know this name. It enables me to participate online without being subject to harassment that at one point in time led to my employer having to change their number so that calls could get through."

- "I do not feel safe using my real name online as I have had people track me down from my online presence and had coworkers invade my private life."

- "I've been stalked. I'm a rape survivor. I am a government employee that is prohibited from using my IRL [Internet relay chat]."

- "As a former victim of stalking that impacted my family I've used [my nickname] online for about 7 years."

- "[This name] is a pseudonym I use to protect myself. My web site can be rather controversial and it has been used against me once."

- "I started using [this name] to have at least a little layer of anonymity between me and people who act inappropriately/criminally. I think the 'real names' policy hurts women in particular."

- "I enjoy being part of a global and open conversation, but I don't wish for my opinions to offend conservative and religious people I know or am related to. Also I don't want my husband's Govt career impacted by his opinionated wife, or for his staff to feel in any way uncomfortable because of my views."

- "I have privacy concerns for being stalked in the past. I'm not going to change my name for a google plus page. The price I might pay isn't worth it."

- "We get death threats at the blog, so while I'm not all that concerned with, you know, sane people finding me. I just don't overly share information and use a pen name."

- "This identity was used to protect my real identity as I am gay and my family live in a small village where if it were openly known that their son was gay they would have problems."

- "I go by pseudonym for safety reasons. Being female, I am wary of Internet harassment."

You'll notice a theme here. . . .

Real Names and the Marginalized

Another site has popped up called "My Name Is Me" where people vocalize their support for pseudonyms. What's most striking is the list of people who are affected by "real names" policies, including abuse survivors, activists, LGBT [lesbian, gay, bisexual, and transgender] people, women, and young people.

Over and over again, people keep pointing to Facebook as an example where "real names" policies work. This makes me laugh hysterically. One of the things that became patently clear to me in my fieldwork is that countless teens who signed up to Facebook late into the game chose to use pseudonyms or nicknames. What's even more noticeable in my data is that an extremely high percentage of people of color used pseudonyms as compared to the white teens that I interviewed. Of course, this would make sense. . . .

The people who most heavily rely on pseudonyms in online spaces are those who are most marginalized by systems of power. "Real names" policies aren't empowering; they're an authoritarian assertion of power over vulnerable people. These ideas and issues aren't new, but what is new is that marginalized people are banding together and speaking out loudly. And thank goodness.

Facebook and Google Plus

What's funny to me is that people also don't seem to understand the history of Facebook's "real names" culture. When early adopters (first the elite college students . . .) embraced Facebook, it was a trusted community. They gave the name that they used in the context of college or high school or the corporation that they were a part of. They used the name that fit into the network that they joined Facebook with. The names they used weren't necessarily their legal names; plenty of people chose Bill instead of William. But they were, for all intents and purposes, "real." As the site grew larger, people had to grapple with new crowds being present and discomfort emerged over the norms. But the norms were set and people kept signing up and giving the name that they were most commonly known by. By the time celebrities kicked in, Facebook wasn't demanding that Lady Gaga call herself Stefani Germanotta, but of course, she had a "fan page" and was separate in the eyes of the crowd. Meanwhile, what many folks failed to notice is that countless black and Latino youth signed up to Facebook using handles. Most people don't notice what black and Latino youth do online. Likewise, people from outside of the US started signing up to Facebook and using alternate names. Again, no one noticed because names transliterated from Arabic or Malaysian or containing phrases in Portuguese weren't particularly visible to the real-name enforcers. Real names are by no means universal on Facebook, but . . . the importance of real names is a myth that Facebook likes to shill out. And, for the most part, privileged white Americans use their real names on Facebook. So it "looks" right.

Then along comes Google Plus, thinking that it can just dictate a "real names" policy. Only, they made a huge mistake. They allowed the tech crowd to join within 48 hours of launching. The thing about the tech crowd is that it has a long history of nicks and handles and pseudonyms. And this crowd got to define the early social norms of the site, rather than being socialized into the norms set up by trusting college students who had joined a site that they thought was college-only. This was not a recipe for "real name" norm setting. Quite the opposite. Worse for Google . . . tech folks are VERY happy to speak LOUDLY when they're pissed off. So while countless black and Latino folks have been using nicks all over Facebook (just like they did on Myspace [another social media site] btw), they never loudly challenged Facebook's policy. There was more of a "live and let live" approach to this. Not so lucky for Google and its name-bending community. Folks are now PISSED OFF.

Changes in Online Anonymity

Because users are fundamentally disembodied when communicating via digital media, they also have the potential to be as anonymous as they wish to be. Indeed, the Internet was originally touted as a place where one could leave one's body behind. To some extent, this was true during the early days of the Internet. Because of the nature of technology (lower bandwidth, no images or video), the nature of the applications that were available (e.g., chat rooms, bulletin boards), and the fact that the Internet was not very diffuse, one was not as likely to meet and interact with friends and acquaintances while online. Anonymity on the Internet is much more complex today—users can choose to be anonymous on applications, such as bulletin boards and virtual worlds such as Second Life. However, anonymity may be virtually impossible on applications like social networking sites, where cues about the body and the self are readily available, and where teens may be more likely to interact with people whom they already know off-line. Nevertheless, even when one is supposedly not anonymous, users can nonetheless fabricate their online identity or embellish parts of an otherwise true off-line identity. Finally, online anonymity is hard to achieve, as every device on an online network has a public IP [Internet protocol] address, and one needs to be technologically sophisticated to hide or mask an IP address.

Kaveri Subrahmanyam and David Smahel,
Digital Youth: The Role of Media in Development.
New York: Springer, 2011, p. 14.

The Right to Protect Themselves

Personally, I'm ecstatic to see this much outrage. And I'm really really glad to see seriously privileged people take up the issue, because while they are the least likely to actually be harmed by "real names" policies, they have the authority to be able to speak truth to power. And across the web, I'm seeing people highlight that this issue has more depth to it than fun names (and is a whole lot more complicated than boiling it down to being about anonymity, as Facebook's Randi Zuckerberg foolishly did).

What's at stake is people's right to protect themselves, their right to actually maintain a form of control that gives them safety. If companies like Facebook and Google are actually committed to the safety of their users, they need to take these complaints seriously. Not everyone is safer by giving out their real name. Quite the opposite; many people are far LESS safe when they are identifiable. And those who are least safe are often those who are most vulnerable.

Likewise, the issue of reputation must be turned on its head when thinking about marginalized people. Folks point to the issue of people using pseudonyms to obscure their identity and, in theory, "protect" their reputation. The assumption baked into this is that the observer is qualified to actually assess someone's reputation. All too often, and especially with marginalized people, the observer takes someone out of context and judges them inappropriately based on what they get online. Let me explain this in a concrete example that many of you have heard before. Years ago, I received a phone call from an Ivy League college admissions officer who wanted to accept a young black man from South Central in LA into their college; the student had written an application about how he wanted to leave behind the gang-ridden community he came from, but the admissions officers had found his Myspace which was filled with gang insignia. The question that was asked of me was "Why would he lie to us when we can tell the truth online?" Knowing that community, I was fairly certain that he was being honest with the college; he was also doing what it took to keep himself alive in his community. If he had used a pseudonym, the college wouldn't have been able to get data out of context about him and inappropriately judge him. But they didn't. They thought that their frame mattered most. I really hope that he got into that school.

There is no universal context, no matter how many times geeks want to tell you that you can be one person to everyone at every point. But just because people are doing what it takes to be appropriate in different contexts, to protect their safety, and to make certain that they are not judged out of context doesn't mean that everyone is a huckster. Rather, people are responsibly and reasonably responding to the structural conditions of these new media. And there's nothing acceptable about those who are most privileged and powerful telling those who aren't that it's OK for their safety to be undermined. And you don't guarantee safety by stopping people from using pseudonyms, but you do undermine people's safety by doing so.

Thus, from my perspective, enforcing "real names" policies in online spaces is an abuse of power.

Periodical and Internet Sources Bibliography

The following articles have been selected to supplement the diverse views presented in this chapter.

Marcus Daniel	"Are We Less Civil Now?," Zócalo Public Square, July 12, 2012.
Robert Eisinger	"Internet Incivility: Possibilities for Engaging Students?," *Huffington Post*, October 20, 2011.
Cal FitzSimmons	"Anonymous Comments Can Lead to Incivility," *Wenatchee World* (Washington State), April 1, 2011.
Leslie Harris and Emma J. Llanso	"Facebook Age and Anonymity: Civility vs. Freedom of Speech," ABC News, June 2, 2011.
David Harsanyi	"Harsanyi: Civility Is Overrated," Denverpost.com, September 18, 2009.
Ki Mae Heussner	"Are You Your Avatar? Book Details Dangers of the 'E-Personality,'" ABC News, January 27, 2011.
Donna Leinwand Leger	"Internet Creates Wider Venue for Political Incivility, Threats," *USA Today*, February 2, 2012.
Bill Reader	"Free Press vs. Free Speech? The Rhetoric of 'Civility' in Regard to Anonymous Online Comments," *Journalism and Mass Communication Quarterly*, May 22, 2012.
Justine Roberts	"We Should Protect the Right to Web Anonymity, Says Mumsnet Chief," *Guardian*, February 15, 2012.
Alina Tugend	"Incivility Can Have Costs Beyond Hurt Feelings," *New York Times*, November 19, 2010.

Chapter 2

Is Cyberbullying a Serious Problem?

Chapter Preface

Cyberbullying, or systematic online harassment, has garnered much attention among schools and policy makers. Researchers have attempted to determine who is vulnerable to cyberbullying and who perpetrates it. In this context, they have investigated whether cyberbullying is more prevalent among girls or boys.

A September 2, 2010, article by Gregg MacDonald in the *Washington Post* reports on research suggesting that girls are more at risk of cyberbulling than are boys. MacDonald reports on a study by researchers at Florida Atlantic University that found that girls were more likely to be cyberbullies, more likely to be the victims of cyberbullying, and more likely to report cyberbullying to their parents than were their male peers.

The study also found that boys and girls tend to participate in different kinds of cyberbullying. The researchers found that "girls are more likely to spread rumors, while boys are more likely to post hurtful pictures or videos."

However, other studies have reached very different conclusions. In a July 28, 2011, article the *Scotsman* reports that researchers had found that *boys*, not girls, were more likely to be cyberbullies and to experience cyberbullying by their peers. The lead researcher, Dr. Sarah Pedersen, found that 68 percent of boys between ten and twenty-one said they had been bullied, compared to only 49 percent of girls. Similarly, 50 percent of boys said they had committed cyberbullying compared to only 33 percent of girls. Pedersen also found that boys were more likely than girls to be the victims of "Frape," or Facebook rape. Frape occurs when a person is logged into Facebook and steps away from the computer, giving someone else a chance to change the settings and profile in ways designed to embarrass or humiliate the user.

Pedersen suggested that the greater number of boys bullying and being bullied may in part be a result of the fact that anti-cyberbullying programs have tended to target girls. Since girls have been perceived as being more at risk, they have been the focus of online safety campaigns. "Girls seem to be much more clued up on the whole idea of privacy and being careful online," Pedersen said. "The message seems to have got through to them because they are doing something right. But we need to get the message through to the boys as well."

The rest of this chapter discusses other controversies and debates surrounding the nature and dangers of cyberbullying.

> "The most important first step an employer can take to deal with cyberbullying is to create awareness about it in the workplace."

Cyberbullying in the Workplace Is a Growing Problem

Erica Pinsky

Erica Pinsky is a workplace solutions expert and the author of Road to Respect: Path to Profit. *In the following viewpoint, she says that cyberbullying is a growing problem in the workplace. She says that cyberbullying, like regular bullying in the workplace, is designed to embarrass or harm and to publicly humiliate. She says it is accomplished through technology, which can allow for anonymity and make it more difficult to stop. She concludes that employers should have specific policies in place to stop and address cyberbullying. She also says employers should work with information technology departments to monitor employee activity online.*

As you read, consider the following questions:

1. What does Pinsky say that cyberbullying is about, and what does she say motivates it?

Erica Pinsky, "Cyber-Bullying: The Latest Weapon in the Hands of Workplace Bullies," Human Resources IQ, September 22, 2010. http://www.humanresourcesiq.com. Copyright © 2010 by Erica Pinsky. All rights reserved. Reproduced by permission.

2. According to Pinsky, what are some ways that a cyber-bully can use technology to reach his or her target?

3. What should employees be advised to do to fight cyber-bullying, according to Pinsky?

Imagine arriving at work to find an angry manager at your door, waving an e-mail she got from one of her team at you and demanding that this ungrateful and disrespectful employee be fired. A quick glance at the e-mail gets your blood boiling even before you've had a coffee—it is filled with insults and denigrating comments. To make matters worse you see it has been cc:d to the entire executive team.

Tools for Bullies

You do your best to calm the manager down and then arrange to meet with the employee. A quick look at her employee file reveals that she is a long-standing employee with a stellar performance record, recently promoted into her current position. It is quickly apparent that something doesn't add up.

Your suspicions are confirmed when the employee arrives at your office. You hand her the e-mail and her face registers shock. She looks up at you and says, "I didn't send this!"

The advent of Web 2.0 has created a smorgasbord of new tools for those interested in promoting workplace disrespect, damaging relationships, and destroying reputations. Cyber-bullying, sometimes referred to as cyber-harassment, is a growing problem in today's workplaces, and one that HR [human resources] professionals should be equipped to deal with.

According to the National Crime Prevention Council, cyber-bullying occurs "when the Internet, cell phones or other devices are used to send or post text or images intended to hurt or embarrass another person." Wikipedia defines it as "when someone repeatedly makes fun of another person online or repeatedly picks on another person through e-mails or text messages, or uses online forums and postings online intended to harm, damage, humiliate or isolate another person that they don't like."

Like traditional workplace bullying, cyber-bullying is about power and control in workplace relationships. It is often motivated by insecurity, jealousy or fear. The intention of the perpetrator is the same: to undermine, discredit, embarrass and/or harm the target through sabotage, insults, undermining work performance, public humiliation, and sarcasm. The main difference is the use of technology to accomplish this goal.

And that technology can make quite a difference. As illustrated in the example above, cyber-bullies can hide their actions under a cloak of anonymity and do far-reaching damage with just one text, post or e-mail message. They can reach their targets outside the workplace, in their homes, or cars through cell phones and PDAs [personal digital assistants]. They are able to block their numbers, use an alias, or access someone else's e-mail address so that a target may have no idea where the message is originating. A disgruntled employee can now choose to target his/her employer by anonymously posting damaging or even privileged information about the company to social media sites, blogs or chat rooms, rival companies or to traditional media.

Research shows that workplace bullying affects a significant number of employees, and is no longer an issue that employers, or HR business leaders, can afford to ignore. Cyber-bullying is one aspect of this growing problem that is costing employers billions of dollars. Productivity, teamwork and creativity are destroyed, while absenteeism, turnover and conflict increase.

Create Awareness, Establish a Policy

As with traditional bullying, the most important first step an employer can take to deal with cyber-bullying is to create awareness about it in the workplace. Make sure that employ-

Growth in Online Bullying at Work

Officially reported incidences of bullying and cyber bullying in workplace settings are comparatively rare to nonwork bullying situations, although some researchers believe rates of workplace bullying is "alarming." If this is true, the reasons are probably due to a combination of youth having grown up among cyber incivility entering workforces that steadily rely on . . . IT [information technology] devices they . . . are more accustomed to using. So just as traditional bullying has found its way into cyber forms on the Internet, so too has school-yard bullying transcended into employment settings where adults work.

Samuel C. McQuade III, James P. Colt, and Nancy B.B. Meyer,
Cyber Bullying: Protecting Kids and Adults from Online Bullies.
Westport, CT: Praeger, 2009, p. 182.

ees know what it is, how to recognize it, and what to do when they encounter it. Add clear language about bullying, including cyber-bullying to existing antiharassment policies, and ensure that employees understand the consequences of engaging in this kind of disrespectful behavior. Establish an acceptable use policy (AUP) related to Internet technology. Make it a part of employee orientation to ensure that employees understand what it means and have them sign off on it.

One advantage in dealing with cyber-bullying over traditional bullying, which so often happens in private, is that it is occurring in a public domain. E-mails, text messages, posts to blogs or social media sites can be saved to determine if the origin can be traced. Employers should work closely with their IT [information technology] departments, to develop a strategy and techniques to control and monitor what employees are doing online, which can include running reports on web access. Employees should be advised to create a safe-sender list to block anonymous messages and to immediately report anything that breaches corporate Internet protocol.

Success in today's challenging business climate requires adaptability and responsiveness to our new realities. Take proactive measures to make your workplace a "cyber-bullying free zone" and reap the possibilities offered by technology to promote respect and connectedness in your workplace.

> *"Online bullying is not only driving ordinary youth to suicide, but anonymous trolls are celebrating those deaths in what could only be equated to the chatroom equivalent of snuff videos."*

Cyberbullying Among Students Is a Dangerous Epidemic

Isabeau Doucet

Isabeau Doucet is a writer whose work has appeared in the Guardian, Nation, and on Al Jazeera. In the following viewpoint, she reports on the growing prevalence and cruelty of online harassment and bullying. She points to incidents in which bullied teens committed suicide. She also highlights incidents in which online bullies have targeted families of those whose loved ones have died, defacing tribute pages and harassing grieving relatives. Doucet argues that the police capacity to stop trolls, or those who harass others online, is insufficient, and she concludes that cyberbullying is causing serious and increasing damage.

Isabeau Doucet, "Anti-Social Network: The Rise of a Cyber-Bullying Epidemic," The Bureau of Investigative Journalism, March 20, 2012. http://www.thebureauinvestigates.com. Copyright © 2012 by The Bureau of Investigative Journalism. All rights reserved. Reproduced by permission.

As you read, consider the following questions:

1. According to Doucet, who was Tom Mullaney, and how did cyberbullying affect him?

2. What does Doucet say prompted Richard Bacon to create a documentary about trolling and cyberbullying?

3. What statistics does Carney Bonner cite to show the prevalence of cyberbullying?

"It all started, I was just on Facebook when I was drunk" said Damon Richards, a notorious cyber troll [referring to someone who harasses others online] who cut his teeth in the world of online bullying by photoshopping a picture of singer Susan Boyle replacing the microphone with a penis. Having a laugh online "can be slightly addictive," he admits to presenter Richard Bacon in the BBC documentary *The Anti-Social Network*, and it can degenerate into a terrifying new breed of twenty-first-century psychos called "RIP trolls."

Tom Mullaney was a lively 15-year-old boy with no history of being bullied, but all it took to shred his world apart was one night with 12 threatening Facebook messages from 6 of his classmates. His father found him in the shed at the back of the garden, hanged. He was cyber-lynched to suicide. After the devastated Mullaney family set up an online tribute page in Tom's loving memory, the site went viral in the RIP troll community and they swiftly desecrated it with a barrage of nasty comments—"cold and stiff"—and photoshopped images of Tom with a lasso around his neck, or his decapitated head in a sliced sausage with caption "RIP Tom Baloney."

The Power of the Written Word

With a camera framed tightly around his face, Damond Richards is confronted with nasty homosexual comments left on Tom Mullaney's RIP site by one of his online aliases. What do the micro-expressions twitching in his brow reveal? Does he

"An angry man with his angry keyboard," cartoon by Tim Cordell, www.CartoonStock .com.

understand the emotional damage caused by his comments? Would he be capable of uttering those words in person to Mullaney's family? Would they be as hurtful in person or is the destructiveness of trolling the very fact that written words, magnified by the Internet for all to see, hold special powers? Should such abuse, keyboard-clicked into cyber-space, qualify as a hate crime? How can the murky line between freedom of speech, boorish teasing and suicide-inducing insults be defined by laws? These are all urgent ethical questions for an era where slow-moving laws fail utterly to keep up with fast-evolving technology.

Online bullying from peers is not only driving ordinary youth to suicide, but anonymous trolls are celebrating those deaths in what could only be equated to the chat-room equivalent of snuff videos. While it's hardly surprising to see school-yard bullying migrate to Facebook, RIP trolling is something darker, weirder and possibly a symptom of some new 21st-century cyber-induced psychosis.

RIP trolls, according to a "troll hunter" interviewed anonymously in this documentary, daily scour the papers and Internet for news of dead children and babies, and if there's no RIP page on which to shower abuse—often obscene and sexually explicit—they'll set one up for the purpose.

For over two years, Richard Bacon has had an obsessive cyber-stalker who disseminates his darkest, most hateful fantasies about the TV and radio personality's death via anonymous Twitter and Facebook accounts. When the troll started attacking Bacon's wife and newborn child, he decided to try and hunt him down and make a documentary about why Britain's trolls seem to have recently gone into overdrive. Bacon interviews a wide array of voices: teenage girls who have had to go on medication, parents who have lost their children, celebrities who fought back and were flooded with solidarity, counsellors, psychiatrists, and people who have taken it upon themselves to fill in for the lack of regulation and accountability online.

The Prevalence of Cyber-Bullying

Cyber-bullying is a lot more common than might be expected, according to Carney Bonner who runs a mentoring and support group. The statistics are that "one in three people aged between 11 to 17 are cyber bullied, with girls three times more likely. It goes to school with you, it comes home with you, it goes in the shower with you, it goes everywhere you go."

What this programme shows is that more than half of cyber-stalkers know their victims personally, but the Internet has opened up myriad of sophisticated ways of hiding your identity, or stealing that of others, and the police's investigative capabilities are lagging woefully behind. With the help of the BBC's Internet research specialist, Paul Myers, Bacon sets up a honey trap to lure his troll into divulging his identity. Bacon effectively self-trolls, pretending to be someone else tweeting abuse at himself and offering to send the troll compromising pictures of himself in hopes of sweet-talking his troll into contact.

Disappointingly Bacon fails to entrap his troll, but he does doorstep one of the only two convicted (under the 2003 communications act) trolls in Britain, who is allegedly still at it after serving 18 months in prison. If hiding identity online is the *modus operandi* of trolling, seeing a troll squirm in the flesh as Bacon and his camera crew confront him with printed screenshots of his hateful drivel makes for extremely satisfying TV.

"*Exaggerating bullying makes it . . . [seem] like it's normal: 'Everyone does it so it must be OK.'*"

Cyberbullying Among Students Is Serious, but It Is Not an Epidemic

Larry Magid

Larry Magid is codirector of ConnectSafely.org and founder of SafeKids.com. In the following viewpoint, he argues that cyberbullying is a serious problem, but it is not an unstoppable epidemic. On the contrary, he says that statistics show incidents of bullying and teen suicide are decreasing. He argues that exaggerating the threat of bullying may make bullying seem more normal and may actually lead more individuals to bully. Instead, he argues that parents should be calm and act to stop cyberbullying without overreacting or exaggerating the problem.

As you read, consider the following questions:

1. Why does Magid say that cyberbullying statistics can vary widely?

Larry Magid, "Cyberbullying Is a Serious Problem, but Is It an Epidemic?," *Huffington Post*, September 17, 2011. Copyright © 2011 by Larry Magid. All rights reserved. Reproduced by permission.

2. What does Magid say is the most commonly recognized definition of bullying?

3. According to Magid, why should parents not take away Internet privileges from a child who is being cyberbullied?

I'm glad that media outlets and public officials are shining a light on cyberbullying and bullying in general. It's important to pay attention to this serious problem, but we need to keep it in perspective. As bad as it is, cyberbullying is not an epidemic and it's not killing our children.

Assessing Risk

Yes, it's probably one of the more widespread youth risks on the Internet and yes there are some well-publicized horrific cases of cyberbullying victims who have committed suicide, but let's look at this in context.

Bullying has always been a problem among adolescents and, sadly, so has suicide. In the few known cases of suicide after cyberbullying, there are likely other contributing factors. That's not to diminish the tragedy or suggest that the cyberbullying didn't play a role but—as with all online youth risk—we need to look at what else was going on in the child's life. Even when a suicide or other tragic event does occur, cyberbullying is often accompanied by a pattern of off-line bullying and sometimes there are other issues including depression, problems at home, and self-esteem issues.

"Suicide," said psychologist Dr. Patti Agatston, "is a complex and multifaceted act that is the result of a combination of factors in any individual. What we need to learn more about is what are the protective factors, since many youth are bullied and do not engage in suicidal behaviors." Agatston is a board member of the International Bullying Prevention Association (IBPA) that's planning an upcoming conference themed "Bullying and Intolerance: From Risk to Resiliency."

Bullying and Teen Suicide
Are Not Increasing

While there is increased awareness of the dangers of bullying and rightful concern over suicide, the percentage of youth who report being physically bullied actually decreased between 2003 and 2008 from 22% to 15%, according to a peer-reviewed study published in the *Archives of Pediatrics & Adolescent Medicine*. And before making any assumptions about technology contributing to teen suicide, take a look at government data that shows (with the exception of 2004) a slight gradual decline in teen suicide rates from the 1990s to 2008.

Certain populations—especially gay, lesbian, [bisexual] and transgender (LGBT) youth, experience a significantly higher rate of bullying. An Iowa State University study found that 54% of LGBT youth had been victims of cyberbullying within the past 30 days. 45% of the respondents "reported feeling depressed as a result of being cyberbullied," according to the study's authors. 38% felt embarrassed, and 28% felt anxious about attending school. The authors reported that "more than a quarter (26%) had suicidal thoughts."

Research from the Cyberbullying Research Center indicates that about one in five teens have been cyberbullied at least once in their lifetimes and 10% in the past 30 days. That's bad, but not an epidemic. A 2010 study by Cox Communications came up with numbers similar to those from the Cyberbullying Research Center, finding that approximately 19 percent of teens say they've been cyberbullied online or via text message and 10 percent say they've cyberbullied someone else. Partly because there is no single accepted definition of cyberbullying, you will find other numbers that are much higher and much lower.

One thing we know about cyberbullying is that it's often associated with real-world bullying. A UCLA [University of California, Los Angeles] study found that 85 percent of those bullied online were also bullied at school.

It may seem counterintuitive but research has shown that exaggeration and scare tactics can actually increase risk.... Exaggerating bullying makes it ... [seem] like it's normal: "Everyone does it so it must be OK." Norms research from professors H. Wesley Perkins and David Craig has shown that emphasizing that most kids don't bully actually decreases bullying. As Cyberbullying Research Center codirector Justin [W.] Patchin said in my CBS News/CNET podcast, kids have a tendency to way overestimate the percentage of kids who bully.... When reporting on suicide risk, it's important for media to study guidelines and be sensitive to risk of copycat suicides.

Cyberbullying Defined

The most commonly recognized definition of bullying includes repeated, unwanted aggressive behavior over a period of time with an imbalance of power between the bully and the victim. In theory, that also covers cyberbullying, but some have taken a broader approach to cyberbullying to also include single or occasional episodes of a person insulting another person online. Indeed, because of the possibility of it being forwarded, a single episode of online harassment can have long-term consequences. "'Power' and 'repetition' may be manifested a bit differently online than in traditional bullying," Susan Limber, professor of psychology at Clemson University, said in an interview that appeared in a publication of the U.S. Department of Education's Office of Safe and Drug-Free Schools. She added, "a student willing to abuse technology can easily wield great power over his or her target just by having the ability to reach a large audience, and often by hiding his or her identity."

Manifestations of cyberbullying include name-calling, sending embarrassing pictures, sharing personal information or secrets without permission, and spreading rumors. It can also include trickery, exclusion, and impersonation.

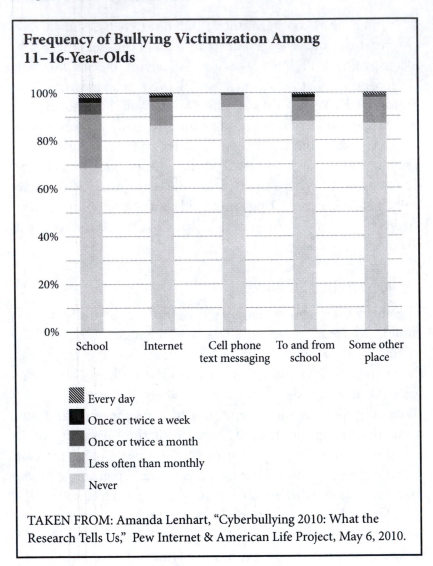

Frequency of Bullying Victimization Among 11–16-Year-Olds

Legend:
- Every day
- Once or twice a week
- Once or twice a month
- Less often than monthly
- Never

TAKEN FROM: Amanda Lenhart, "Cyberbullying 2010: What the Research Tells Us," Pew Internet & American Life Project, May 6, 2010.

Some have a much broader definition of cyberbullying that can include any type of mean or rude comment, even if it's not particularly hurtful or traumatic.

When talking about bullying and cyberbullying, it's important to remember that not every incident is equally harmful. There are horrendous cases where children are terribly hurt but there are many cases where kids are able to handle it themselves. That's not to say it's ever right—there is never an excuse for being mean—but parents and authorities need to avoid jumping to immediate conclusions until they understand the severity of an incident. And, of course, different children will react differently to incidents depending on a number of factors including their own physiological makeup, vulnerability, and resiliency.

It's not always obvious if a child is a victim of cyberbullying, but some possible signs include suddenly being reluctant to go online or use a cell phone; avoiding a discussion about what they're doing online; depression, mood swings, change in eating habits; and aloofness or a general disinterest in school and activities. A child closing the browser or turning off the cell phone when a parent walks in the room can be a sign of cyberbullying, though it can also be a sign of other issues including an inappropriate relationship or just insistence on privacy.

There are no silver bullets but at ConnectSafely.org (a site I help operate) we came up with a number of tips including don't respond, don't retaliate; talk to a trusted peer or adult; and save the evidence. We also advise young people to be civil toward others and not to be bullies themselves. Finally, "be a friend, not a bystander." Don't forward mean messages and let bullies know that their actions are not cool.

If your child is cyberbullied, don't start by taking away his or her Internet privileges. That's one reason kids often don't talk about net-related problems with parents. Instead, try to get your child to calmly explain what has happened. If possible, talk with the parents of the other kids involved and, if necessary, involve school authorities. If the impact of the bullying spills over to school (as it usually does), the school has a right to intervene to protect the [child].

> *"The furor is not overblown, and we do need federal laws to stop cyber bullying, harassment and abuse."*

Anti-Cyberbullying Laws Are Needed to Fight Cyberbullying

Ben Leichtling

Ben Leichtling is the author of Bullies Below the Radar, How to Stop Bullies in Their Tracks, *and* Eliminate the High Cost of Low Attitudes. *In the following viewpoint, he argues that federal laws are needed to protect children from cyberbullying. He says that the threat of cyberbullying is not exaggerated. He adds that even if cyberbullying laws would raise some difficulties, providing some protection for the bullied is better than providing no protection. He concludes that laws set standards of conduct, and he argues that law enforcement needs to evolve to keep up with technology.*

As you read, consider the following questions:

1. How does Leichtling respond to the claim that peer-to-peer off-line bullying is more of a threat than cyberbullying?

Ben Leichtling, "Federal Laws Needed to Stop Cyber Bullying, Harassment and Abuse," Blogger News Network, July 8, 2009. Copyright © 2009 by Ben Leichtling. All rights reserved. Reproduced by permission.

2. What does Leichtling say to the idea that cyberbullying can best be solved through education?

3. According to Leichtling, on what understanding are our laws founded?

According to the *Wall Street Journal,* a recent report on cyber bullying suggests that, unlike other Internet scares, this one is well founded, but it questions some of the regulatory efforts that are gathering steam. The report, by the Progress & Freedom Foundation, a right-leaning Washington think tank that focuses on technology public policy, says that data from child-safety researchers indicate that much of the furor is overblown.

Protections Are Needed

I disagree strongly: The furor is not overblown, and we do need federal laws to stop cyber bullying, harassment and abuse.

The right-leaning think tank's objections to new anti–cyber bullying laws are that:

- *Worries over online predators are overblown* because one study of arrests from 2000 to 2006 showed that most of the offenders approached undercover investigators, not kids. I'm glad the offenders approached undercover investigators. But that's no reason not to have laws. Between 2006 and now, offenders have gotten smarter. And, of course we want laws so we can protect the kids who are approached.

- *They estimate that threats due to peer-to-peer bullying are more serious than those due to cyber bullying.* Even if that's true, that's no reason to abandon kids who are targets of cyber bullying, harassment and abuse. As shown by the case of Lori Drew, without federal laws, cyber bullies can't be prosecuted effectively. The judge acquitted this adult even though she set up the My-space site that was used to harass and abuse teenager Megan Meier until she committed suicide.

- *Laws pose "thorny issues" that are entwined with free speech.* Again, that's no reason not to enter the thicket. That simply lets us know that the laws will have gray areas and both the law and the interpretations will be continuously evolving as hardened criminals find loop-holes. Laws encourage angry, potentially vindictive people to think twice before doing anything impulsive and rash.

- *Laws would make statements that defame, embarrass, harm, abuse, threaten, slander or harass third parties illegal online,* even though such statements would be allowed if said on a playground. That's not a problem; that's an obvious benefit. That acknowledges the truism that statements made in a local context or face-to-face usually have very different consequences than hostility put out to the whole world on the Internet, especially if the statements are anonymous or made through the safety of false identities.

- *We can solve the problem best through better education.* Nonsense. Of course, education and vigorous stop-bullies programs are very helpful, but they're not enough. Education alone does not yield the most ben-efits. Education, anti-bullying programs and enforced laws all together yield the most benefits.

- *Teaching people to behave civilly online is no different than teaching children to use proper table manners, to cover their mouths when they sneeze or to say, "thank you."* That's also nonsense. If an adult is a slob at home, no one else is harmed. If someone gets drunk and disruptive at a restaurant, a movie theater or a ball game, they can be asked to leave or ejected or arrested. The harm caused by eating with the wrong fork or not saying "please" or "thank you" is minor compared to the harm that can be caused by cyber bullying, harassment or abuse. Ask the families of Megan Meier or Jessica Logan, both of whom committed suicide after they were made the targets of cyber bullying. Ask the families of the thousands we don't hear about in the media. They suffer, helpless to stop their abusers, but valiantly and quietly to struggle through life.

Laws Set Standards

Online attacks are becoming an epidemic. Some sites even specialize as forums for anonymous bashing and attacks.

Laws are made to state the standards to which we aspire and to diminish people's ability to harm others as much as possible. Laws may be imperfect and enforcement may be difficult and spotty, but that's better than nothing. I'd rather have anti-bullying laws that protect kids 90% of the time and have difficulties 10% of the time, than have no laws to stop cyber bullying and leave kids vulnerable 100% of the time.

Our laws and even our system of checks and balances are founded on our understanding that no matter how much education people have, they will often seek power and revenge. They won't always be good and sweet and kind. If given the chance, people will be mean, nasty and vicious to others, especially if they can act anonymously or the target can't fight back effectively.

We must rise to the challenge posed by new technology and keep evolving laws and enforcing them the best we can.

> *"Anti–cyber bullying laws are the greatest threat to student free speech because they seek to censor it everywhere and anytime it occurs."*

Anti-Cyberbullying Laws Are a Threat to Free Speech

John O. Hayward

John O. Hayward is a senior lecturer in law at Bentley University. In the following viewpoint, he argues that cyberbullying laws are often vague and broad. As such, they prohibit students from engaging in controversial speech, whether on school grounds or off school grounds. Therefore, he says, these violate the First Amendment. He says that most cyberbullying laws will be struck down on constitutional grounds. He concludes that students should have broad free speech rights in schools as preparation for participation in vigorous democratic debate.

As you read, consider the following questions:

1. According to Hayward, anti-cyberbullying statutes contain language prohibiting cyberbullying if it has one or more of what six results?

John O. Hayward, "Anti–Cyber Bullying Statutes Threat to Student Free Speech," *Selected Works of John O. Hayward*, September 2010, pp. 3–34. Copyright © 2010 by John O. Hayward. All rights reserved. Reproduced by permission.

2. What was the Chihuahua Haters of America, and what happened to its organizer, according to Hayward?

3. What problems does Hayward point out with the language in New Hampshire's anti-cyberbullying law?

On October 17, 2006, Megan Meier, a thirteen-year-old girl in Dardenne Prairie, Missouri, who had been diagnosed with attention deficit disorder and depression, committed suicide because of postings on Myspace, an Internet social networking site, saying she was a bad person, whom everyone hated and the world would be better off without. As a result, the state revised its harassment and stalking statutes to prohibit using electronic means to knowingly "frighten, intimidate, or cause emotional distress to another person." At the time of this writing, twenty-one states have passed similar legislation with others sure to follow. Many of these statutes were enacted as a result of public hysteria over Megan's death and without due consideration to the threat they pose to freedom of speech. They are intended to combat what has become popularly known as "cyber bullying." This [viewpoint] examines cyber bullying, the laws it has spawned, how they chill student free speech, [and] their constitutionality. . . .

Anti–Cyber Bullying Legislation

While forty-three states have anti-bullying statutes, only twenty-one prohibit cyber bullying, which usually is defined as "bullying" conducted by electronic means. Additionally, the laws can be grouped into prohibitions that explicitly include off-campus cyber bullying or implicitly include or exclude it. Typical legislative language is "immediately adjacent to school grounds," "directed at another student or students," "at a school activity," or "at school-sponsored activities or at a school-sanctioned event."

The statutes also usually contain language prohibiting cyber bullying if it results in one or more of the following: (1)

causes "substantial disruption" of the school environment or orderly operation of the school, (2) creates an "intimidating," "threatening" or "hostile" learning environment, (3) causes actual harm to a student or student's property or places a student in reasonable fear of harm to self or property, (4) interferes with a student's educational performance and benefits, (5) includes as a target school personnel or references "person" rather than "student," and (6) incites third parties to carry out bullying behavior. Five states prohibit cyber bullying if it is motivated by an actual or perceived characteristic or trait of a student. Presumably this protects gay and lesbian students and school personnel from criticism because of their sexual orientation but it could also shield obese, bulimic, short and tall students from disparagement due to their weight or height.

While many applaud anti–cyber bullying legislation, some are concerned that it gives school officials unbridled authority that will be used to burnish their image, not protect bullying victims, or that it threatens student free speech. Furthermore, if their authority is unleashed beyond the school yard, it is essentially limitless. Thus no student, even in the privacy of their home, can write about controversial topics of concern to them without worrying that it may be "disruptive" or cause a "hostile environment" at school. In effect, students will be punished for off-campus speech based on the way people *react* to it at school. Many of the terms are so vague that they offer no guidance to distinguish permissible from impermissible speech. In this sense, they are akin to campus speech codes that courts invalidated in the 1990s for vagueness and overbreadth. Consequently, these laws don't simply "chill" student free speech, they plunge it into deep freeze. This [viewpoint] argues that for these reasons, some anti–cyber bullying laws violate the First Amendment and should be struck down as unconstitutional. . . .

The First Amendment, True Threats and Cyber Bullying

The battle public school officials have been waging against student Internet speech has not gone unnoticed by legal commentators. In one especially egregious example, a 13-year-old boy and his friends created a spoof club called Chihuahua Haters of America and a website called Chihuahua Haters of the World, which contained humorous attacks on Chihuahuas. The student was eventually disciplined for "creating a Web page implicating a Dowell [Middle School] animal hate group." After the ACLU [American Civil Liberties Union] intervened he was reinstated to his computer class and his disciplinary suspension was expunged from his record. While schools have always been able to discipline students for on-campus speech subject to *Tinker*'s "substantial disruption" test,[1] in the pre-Internet and pre-Columbine eras[2] it would have been considered absurd that a school could take disciplinary action against a student for *off-campus* speech. In fact a court in the late 1960s stated that such a result made "little sense." But now the Internet and Columbine are facts of life, so students, school administrators and judges are embroiled in a tug-of-war over student off-campus cyber speech. Most courts confronted with this issue have applied the same legal standards as on-campus speech, which is to say, the "substantial disruption" analysis of *Tinker*. They have ruled that where students create speech off campus but access it on campus, or where it is "reasonably foreseeable" that it will be accessed on campus, they can be disciplined for off-campus speech without violating the First Amendment because substantial disruption is "reasonably foreseeable." . . .

---

1. *Tinker v. Des Moines Independent Community School District* was a case in which students were disciplined for wearing armbands protesting the Vietnam War.
2. Columbine High School was the site of a school shooting by high school students in 1999.

Identifying True Threats

When confronted with cyber bullying in the post-Columbine era, school officials have a difficult task distinguishing "true threats" from student exaggeration, taunting and jokes. In one California case, school officials did not suspend or expel students who admitted posting alleged death threats and anti-gay comments on a student's web site after the police and F.B.I [Federal Bureau of Investigation] investigated and took no action. The parents of the threatened student sued the students who made the posting for intentional infliction of emotional distress, violating their right to be free from threats of violence under the state's hate crime law, and defamation for calling him a homosexual. Several defendants apologized for the postings and said they were intended as "jocular humor." Their motion to have the case thrown out under the state's anti-SLAPP law (Strategic Lawsuit Against Public Participation) was denied along with their claim that the speech was protected under the First Amendment, the California Appeals Court ruling their cyber speech was a "true threat."

Although the California court determined the students' cyber speech to be a true threat, other courts have taken a different view. In *Latour* [referring to *Latour v. Riverside Beaver School District*], the court found that the rap songs created by a middle school student were not true threats. He did not bring any of the songs or recordings to school. They were written in the rap genre and were "just rhymes" and metaphors. Though some of the songs contained violent language, it was violent imagery and he intended no actual violence. He never communicated these songs to the school or to the individuals who were the subjects of the songs. Hence the court enjoined and restrained the school from expelling the student and from banning him from attending school-sponsored events or from being present on school grounds after hours. . . .

Though not involving cyber speech, the court in *Doe v. Pulaski County Special School District* ruled that the student's statements were a true threat. A jilted middle school student drafted two violent, misogynic and obscenity-laden rants expressing a desire to molest, rape and murder his ex-girlfriend. He prepared both letters at his home and never delivered them, but he discussed their contents with her and her friends. One of the friends took the letter with his permission and delivered it to the girl at school at the beginning of a new school year. The school district expelled the boy for the entire school year. The court concluded that the boy intended to communicate the letter and just because he did not personally deliver it did not dispel its threatening nature. The court went on to hold that most, if not all, normal 13-year-old girls (and probably most reasonable adults) would be frightened by the message and tone of the letter and would fear for their physical well-being if they received it. Ruling that the letter was a true threat, the court found that the school did not violate the boy's First Amendment rights by initiating disciplinary action against him.

Vagueness of Laws

Because of their vagueness and overbreadth, it is likely that many anti–cyber bullying statutes will suffer the same fate as campus speech codes and some anti-harassment policies. They share many of their characteristics in seeking to prohibit "hostile environments" and end "intimidating" school speech. They usually contain these phrases along with prohibitions against "interfering with a student's educational performance and benefits" or strictures against comments that are "motivated by actual or perceived characteristics or traits of a student." Whether these expressions encompass simple acts of teasing or name-calling among schoolchildren the courts will have to decide, but the Supreme Court has said they cannot be a basis for damages under federal anti-discrimination law and so it is doubtful they can withstand a First Amendment challenge.

New Hampshire's revised bullying law is a good example of just how far anti-bullying hysteria can go in silencing student free speech. One section reads

> "Bullying" shall include actions motivated by an imbalance of power based on a pupil's actual or perceived personal characteristics, behaviors, or beliefs, or motivated by the pupil's association with another person and based on the other person's characteristics, behaviors, or beliefs.

This certainly takes in a large area of speech that could include teasing someone because they are obese, skinny, tall, short, wear eyeglasses, have long, short or no hair, or speak with a high- or low-pitched voice. One court characterized attempts to prohibit such speech in the context of an anti-harassment policy as "brave, futile, or merely silly." However, the court had harsher words for attempts to censor speech dealing with "beliefs" or "values." To quote:

> But attempting to proscribe negative comments about "values," as that term is commonly used today, is something else altogether. By prohibiting disparaging speech directed at a person's "values," the [anti-harassment] policy strikes at the heart of moral and political discourse—the lifeblood of constitutional self-government (and democratic education) and the core concern of the First Amendment. That speech about "values" may offend is not cause for its prohibition, but rather the reason for its protection: "a principal 'function of free speech under our system of government is to invite dispute. It may indeed best serve its high purpose when it induces a condition of unrest, creates dissatisfaction with conditions as they are, or even stirs people to anger.'" No court or legislature has ever suggested that unwelcome speech directed at another's "values" may be prohibited under the rubric of anti-discrimination.

Undoubtedly suppressing student speech under the guise of preventing "cyber bullying" is no more permissible than attempting to stifle it under the rubric of "anti-harassment." Both run afoul of the First Amendment's guarantee of free speech.

Anti–cyber bullying statutes often include the phrase "hostile environment," words often found in anti-harassment and anti-discrimination codes. The Massachusetts statute defines the phrase as a "situation in which bullying causes the school environment to be permeated with intimidation, ridicule or insult that is sufficiently severe or pervasive to alter the conditions of the student's education." The law does not define "intimidation, ridicule or insult" so students speak to each other at their own peril hoping others won't be "intimidated, ridiculed or insulted" by what they say. This is the essence of what First Amendment jurisprudence terms a "chilling effect" on free speech. It "chills" speech, or makes it less likely that citizens will exercise their rights to free speech because of the fear of criminal punishment. Generally, a statute is unconstitutionally vague if persons "of common intelligence must necessarily guess at its meaning and differ as to its application." Therefore the law has always required "a precise statute 'evincing a legislative judgment that certain specific conduct be . . . proscribed.'" Anti–cyber bullying statutes are replete with terms such as "effect of substantially interfering with a student's education" or "causes emotional distress to a pupil" [a low grade also can cause "emotional distress"]. Anti–cyber bullying laws are more perfidious than speech codes because the latter operate only on school premises whereas many anti–cyber bullying laws seek to regulate student speech off campus.

Overbreadth

Anti–cyber bullying laws, like anti-harassment policies, are not only vulnerable to constitutional challenge based on vagueness but also suffer from overbreadth because they proscribe protected speech as well as unprotected speech.

Free Speech and *Tinker*

The landmark case involving student free speech rights is the case of *Tinker v. [Des] Moines Independent Community School District*. *Tinker* involved a group of high school students who decided to wear black armbands to school to protest the Vietnam War. The court began its opinion by stating that students do not "shed their constitutional rights to freedom of speech or expression at the schoolhouse gate." However, the court acknowledged "the special characteristics of the school environment" by permitting school officials to prohibit student speech if that speech "would substantially interfere with the work of the school or impinge upon the rights of other students," including the right "to be secure." The court upheld the rights of the students to protest because their protest had not created a substantial disruption or interference. However, this standard has been applied at the lower-court level supporting the authority of school officials to respond if student speech has, or if there are good reasons to believe it could, cause a substantial disruption or interference.

Robin M. Kowalski, Susan P. Limber,
and Patricia W. Agatston, Cyberbullying:
Bullying in the Digital Age.
Malden, MA: John Wiley & Sons, 2012, p. 207.

A regulation is unconstitutional on its face on overbreadth grounds where there is "a likelihood that the statute's very existence will inhibit free expression" by "inhibiting the speech of third parties who are not before the Court." To render a law unconstitutional, the overbreadth must be "not only real but substantial in relation to the statute's plainly legitimate sweep." New Hampshire's anti–cyber bullying statute is a good example of overbreadth that has rendered similar language in anti-harassment laws unconstitutional. The law speaks of actions based on a "pupil's actual or perceived personal characteristics." The court in *Saxe* [referring to *Saxe v. State College Area School District*] found such language in an anti-harassment policy to be "facially overbroad" and consequently invalidated the policy. To quote:

> Certainly, some of these purported definitions of harassment are facially overbroad. No one would suggest that a school could constitutionally ban "any unwelcome verbal ... conduct which offends ... an individual" because of "some enumerated personal characteristics." Nor could the school constitutionally restrict, without more, any "unwelcome verbal ... conduct directed at the characteristics of a person's religion." The Supreme Court has held time and again, both within and outside of the school context, that the mere fact that someone might take offense at the content of speech is not sufficient justification for prohibiting it.

The court continues by citing *Texas v. Johnson*:

> If there is a bedrock principle underlying the First Amendment, it is that the government may not prohibit the expression of an idea simply because society finds the idea itself offensive or disagreeable.

The *Saxe* court then applies the *Tinker* "substantial disruption" test to the anti-harassment policy and concludes that it covers substantially more speech than could be prohibited under that rule. Accordingly it held the policy constitutionally overbroad.

Much of the anti–cyber bullying legislation suffers from the same flaw. Without any evidence whatsoever, these statutes proceed to ban vast categories of speech that could not be prohibited under *Tinker*. The Supreme Court made it clear in that case that "undifferentiated fear or apprehension of disturbance is not enough to overcome the right to freedom of expression." Furthermore, the court has held that a law may be invalidated as overbroad if "a substantial number of its applications are unconstitutional, judged in relation to the statute's plainly legitimate sweep." In prohibiting protected speech as well as unprotected speech, anti–cyber bullying statutes are vulnerable to constitutional challenges based on overbreadth.

Just as anti-harassment policies were invalidated for vagueness and overbreadth, many anti–cyber bullying laws will suffer the same fate. . . .

Free Speech for Students

Anti–cyber bullying laws are the greatest threat to student free speech because they seek to censor it everywhere and anytime it occurs, using "substantial disruption" of school activities as justification and often based only on mere suspicion of potential disruption. Although the school environment has special characteristics, they do not justify the regulation of vast areas of student speech unless a "substantial disruption" of school activities can be demonstrated. . . .

As *Tinker* held, students do not shed their constitutional rights to freedom of speech or expression at the schoolhouse gate. Furthermore, if students can't practice free speech in schools, when will they be able to practice it? Certainly not in the workplace, where the First Amendment holds little sway and the atmosphere is apprehensive over potential sexual harassment litigation and its possible expansion to include bullying. Instead of clamping down on student expression, our schools ought to inculcate respect and appreciation for free speech and diverse opinions, the bedrocks of freedom in a democratic society.

> "It almost goes without saying that school districts must educate both students and staff about the harmful nature of online aggression."

Schools and Teachers Can Take Action to Combat Cyberbullying

Sameer Hinduja and Justin W. Patchin

Sameer Hinduja is an assistant professor of criminology at Florida Atlantic University. Justin W. Patchin is an assistant professor of criminal justice at the University of Wisconsin–Eau Claire. In the following viewpoint, the authors argue that the Internet is a valuable educational resource but that children need guidance when accessing and using it. They say that teachers should educate parents and students about online hazards and should provide clear rules for using the Internet and other technology. The authors conclude that schools should cultivate a culture of respect and should take a clear stand against bullying.

As you read, consider the following questions:

1. At what point do the authors suggest that parents should educate children about online risks and dangers?

Sameer Hinduja and Justin W. Patchin, "Preventing Cyberbullying," *Bullying Beyond the Schoolyard: Preventing and Responding to Cyberbullying*, Corwin Press, 2009, pp. 128–141. Copyright © 2009. Reproduced with permission of SAGE Publications, Inc. via Copyright Clearance Center.

2. What is the Ophelia Project, and what resources does it provide?

3. What are some examples of websites and software that the authors suggest might be forbidden at school?

One of the questions we are asked most often when we speak with school professionals, parents, and the media is "How can cyberbullying be prevented?" Indeed, some of you have picked up this book [*Bullying Beyond the Schoolyard: Preventing and Responding to Cyberbullying*, from which this viewpoint is excerpted] solely to figure out the answer to that important question. We devote this chapter to identifying a number of practical approaches that we believe can decrease the frequency of online harassment among youth. While there is no magic bullet to deal with it, there are a number of informed steps that can minimize the likelihood of adolescent aggression in cyberspace. . . .

Students Should Use the Internet

Some suggest that the only way to prevent cyberbullying and some of the other negatives associated with adolescent Internet use is to forbid kids from going online. To be sure, this is the least appropriate course of action. Think about it for a moment. Would you agree that visiting and touring Washington, D.C., would be a fantastic learning opportunity for students? Sure it is: The war memorials, presidential monuments, and governmental buildings are all great places for kids to see and come to appreciate.

Maybe you would like to take the students in your class or school to the nation's capital for a tour. Well, how would you go about it? You certainly wouldn't just drop them off at the steps of the White House and say "Have fun!" You know that in addition to all of the wonderful educational opportunities in Washington, D.C., there are many things you wouldn't necessarily want your students to see: violence, prostitutes, homeless people, drunkards, gang members, and so forth. That urban environment holds a number of dangers; in fact, Washington, D.C., has one of the highest crime rates in the United States. Still, that doesn't mean we should prohibit our students from visiting the city and taking advantage of its historical, political, and cultural attractions.

The Internet should be approached in the same manner. It contains in its seedier corners many things we just don't want our kids to see: foul language, hateful and prejudiced speech, pornography, bomb-making intructions—and the list goes on. The Internet also has many potential dangers: sexual predators, kidnappers, and others with malicious or perverse intent who may want to bring harm to children. Just as we wouldn't leave our kids alone to explore Washington, D.C., we shouldn't leave them alone to explore the Internet without supervision, guidance, and explicit instruction. It is critical to provide them with a clear road map and framework for staying safe and being responsible online and to check in on them regularly to make sure they are following through.

Eventually, all children will be exposed to things in cyberspace that are problematic. What they do at that point depends on the instruction they have received and the habits they have developed. The time, energy, and effort you put in toward this end will pay great dividends in the lives of the youth in whom you invest. While it is not a lost cause to talk to adolescents about appropriate Internet use when they are 17 or 18 years old, so much should be done earlier. We encourage introducing this topic as early as possible—and definitely before they start exploring the Internet alone. We find that between fifth and seventh grade, students begin to use computers and the Internet more often and for more varied purposes, and we have spoken with elementary school children who are vastly more proficient than their teachers and parents. You may not have taught them how to use a computer and the Internet, but they seem to have learned it somewhere.

Kids will undoubtedly become well versed with technology at an increasingly younger age as we move forward in the 21st century. What is encouraging is that adults have a great deal of influence and can meaningfully shape behavior at these earlier ages. You may know from experience that this influence lessens as youth approach the teenage years, so it is vital to step in as soon as possible. This simply means *now*, if it hasn't happened already. We believe that they'll not only hear you speak but actually listen to what you are saying.

A comprehensive strategy to prevent cyberbullying, or any other form of adolescent aggression, requires the cooperation of a number of important stakeholders. Parents, teachers, law enforcement officers, other community leaders, and children themselves all have a role to play. None of these players will be able to do it by themselves. . . .

Teachers and Cyberbullying

It almost goes without saying that school districts must educate both students and staff about the harmful nature of online aggression. School administrators should take the time to learn about these issues and pass this important information along to teachers and counselors. As an example, the district could convene a staff meeting related to youth Internet safety and bring a specialist in to speak on the topic, provide actual case studies, and summarize the latest research findings.

After being so equipped, teachers and counselors need to pass this information on to students. Teachers should take time to discuss cyberbullying in their classrooms when they discuss broader issues of bullying and peer harassment. They should proactively engage students in conversations about a variety of negative online experiences and possible solutions. For instance, teachers can use vignettes or even real examples of cyberbullying to illustrate its harmful nature and point out that what is written or disseminated online is equally as damaging as face-to-face bullying (or worse). . . .

Moreover, we recommend that schools sponsor an assembly or presentation on a regular basis that provides information for the school community about safe and responsible Internet use and "netiquette" (network or online etiquette). To make these presentations more vivid and true to life, we recommend showing hard-hitting video clips related to cyberbullying that are freely available online. For example, the National Crime Prevention Council (www.ncpc.org/cyber bullying) has created public service announcement videos that powerfully portray the real-world harm that online aggression can inflict. The students to whom we have shown these videos are visibly moved as the message sinks in. Repeatedly piquing the consciences of youth about questionable or deviant behavior seems to make them more sensitive to the issues at hand and more apt to "think twice" before making an unwise decision. They should also be deterred to some extent after being reminded of the potential consequences that follow rule breaking and that virtually all forms of wrongdoing online leave a digital footprint that aids in identifying the perpetrator(s).

Several nonprofit organizations have also developed curricula that a school can utilize to educate staff and students about the nature and consequences of cyberbullying. For example, the Anti-Defamation League (ADL) recently launched a nationwide initiative, entitled "Cyberbullying: Understanding and Addressing Online Cruelty," which includes lesson plans for elementary, middle, and secondary school levels. The organization also offers interactive workshops for middle and high school staff. More information about the ADL's cyberbullying programming can be found at www.adl.org.

The Ophelia Project, a nonprofit organization that works with schools to create safer social climates to reduce aggression among students, also provides trainings and workshops for schools about cyberbullying. Their work focuses on combating relational and other nonphysical forms of aggression by promoting emotional well-being and helping youth develop healthy peer relationships. More information can be found at www.opheliaproject.org. Finally, i-SAFE (www.isafe.org) has created an extensive Internet safety curriculum for K–12 youth classrooms and also works to educate community members through comprehensive outreach programs. . . .

Have Clear Rules Regarding the Use of Computers and Other Technological Devices

When we were in seventh-grade "shop" class, we remember spending several weeks at the beginning of the school year studying the safety practices and procedures associated with the power tools before being allowed to use them. Before being permitted to drive a car a couple of years later, we were required to take a comprehensive driver's education course and pass both a written exam and a road test. Society recognizes that power tools and automobiles can be dangerous if used inappropriately or irresponsibly, so we take the time to educate students about the inherent dangers in their operation.

The same approach should be taken before students are allowed to use computers and the Internet at school. Youth cannot be expected to exercise complete wisdom. They need to be taught how to use technology responsibly. Just as there are rules for using power equipment, there should also be clear rules about what is expected when using computers. As long as students know the rules, they cannot plead ignorance if and when they are caught violating them. They should also know the potential consequences for any wrongdoing. . . .

Every school district should have a comprehensive Acceptable Use Policy (AUP) governing the use of technology provided by or used in the schools. The Computer Crime and Intellectual Property Section of the U.S. Department of Justice provides a model AUP, which schools can adapt for their needs. The policy includes detailed information about the safe and responsible use of computers and the Internet and provides suggestions for discipline, supervision, and monitoring. Parents and students must read and sign the AUP (thereby indicating agreement with its terms) at the beginning of every school year. That way, all parties are aware of the policy and the potential consequences associated with any violations of its terms. Interested readers are encouraged to go to www .cybercrime.gov and search for "school acceptable use policy."

In addition to a broad policy, it is also beneficial to post specific principles to guide the behavioral choices of students on computers at school. . . . We also recommend specifying certain web sites and software applications that are forbidden at school (e.g., Myspace, AOL Instant Messenger, Google Talk, and Second Life).

In addition to classroom computer use, students need to know which (if any) portable electronic devices are allowed on campus, as we are seeing a surge in the number of youth who possess laptop computers, smartphones (e.g., iPhones, BlackBerrys, Sidekicks), and other portable electronic devices that are web enabled in some capacity. Coupled with the increasing number of cell phones that provide Internet access, the possibilities for cyberbullying incidents are exponentially rising.

Accordingly, schools must have a clearly defined policy regarding all portable electronic devices. Some schools have simply elected to ban all such devices from campus. These actions have led to criticism by some parents, who say they need to be able to contact their kids in case of an emergency. It can also be very difficult to enforce a complete ban without searching all students as they enter the school each day. A better approach would be to have clearly specified guidelines for when and where the devices are allowed and what will happen if a student is caught using a device at a prohibited time or place. . . .

We would also like to emphasize here that when portable electronic devices are confiscated, schools should not overstep their bounds and search their contents, even when there is a clear violation of school policy. This is best left either to parents or to law enforce, who know when the circumstances call for such an intrusion of privacy. Schools should limit their actions to seizing but not searching these devices.

Anti-Bullying Policies

All schools also have (or should have) policies on the books that prohibit bullying incidents and outline their disciplinary consequences. Administrators must take the time to review and revise them to ensure that they cover cyberbullying behaviors that negatively affect the school environment. This policy should be disseminated at the beginning of the school year so that parents and students understand what behaviors are within the disciplinary reach of the school. It may also be instructive to highlight particular situations that have resulted in disciplinary actions (examples from within the district or elsewhere). As Paul R. Getto, policy specialist for the Kansas Association of School Boards, says,

> The schools need to promote a safe and friendly environment for all students, teachers and other staff, all of whom can be subjected to bullying in many forms, including cyberbullying. Simply passing policies which prohibit bullying is not, in our opinion, going to accomplish the desired results. Bullying in any form, regardless of the media used, is wrong, destructive, and potentially a problem for students and, in some cases, teachers, if they fear for their peace of mind or their safety while in school.

The importance of clear policies is illustrated in a recent example from Florida. In 2007, a middle school student recorded and subsequently uploaded to the Internet (www.youtube.com) video footage of one of her teachers in class and included a profanity-filled caption. Even though there was no substantial disruption of or interference with the school's educational mission, utilization of school-owned technology, or threat to other students, it was within the bounds of the administration to have her transferred to an alternative school, because the school policy expressly forbids the recording of teachers in the classroom.

The policy stated, in part, that "any student who uses an article disruptive to school to inappropriately photograph, audiotape, videotape or otherwise record a person without his/her knowledge or consent will be subject to disciplinary action." We applaud this school for being progressive and forward-thinking enough to have formulated and included such a policy within its conduct manual. It is imperative that other schools and school districts do the same so that the simple and clear violation of a policy prohibiting certain behavior can serve as the basis for punitive sanctions (including changes of placement) by a school on a student. . . .

Maintain a Safe and Respectful School Culture

School culture can be defined as the "sum of the values, cultures, safety practices, and organizational structures within a school that cause it to function and react in particular ways" (J.L. McBrien & R.S. Brandt, 1997). Overall, it is critical for educators to develop and promote a safe and respectful school culture or climate. A positive on-campus environment will go a long way in reducing the frequency of many problematic behaviors at school, including bullying and harassment. In this setting, teachers must demonstrate emotional support, a warm and caring atmosphere, a strong focus on academics and learning, and a fostering of healthy self-esteem.

In our research, we found that students who experienced cyberbullying (both those who were victims and those who admitted to cyberbullying others) perceived a poorer climate or culture at their school than those who had not experienced cyberbullying. Youth were asked whether they "enjoy going to school," "feel safe at school," "feel that teachers at their school really try to help them succeed," and "feel that teachers at their school care about them." Those who admitted to cyberbullying others or who were the target of cyberbullying were less likely to agree with those statements. . . . While we don't know whether a poor school climate *caused* cyberbullying behaviors (or was the result of them), we do know that the variables are related.

In addition, strategic efforts to promote bonding among students should be in place, as this is related to personal, emotional, behavioral, and scholastic success. Toward this end, we often champion what can be termed a "respect policy" or "honor code" when working with schools. For example, one with which we are familiar reads as follows (North High School, 2005):

> Respect is the cornerstone of our relationships with each other. We are committed to respecting the dignity and worth of each individual at North High School and strive never to degrade or diminish any member of our school community by our conduct or attitudes. We benefit from each other. Our diversity makes us strong. . . .

The goal of such a statement is to specify clearly to students and staff alike that all members of the school community are expected to respect each other and that such respect should govern all interpersonal interactions and attitudes among students, faculty, and staff on campus (and hopefully off campus as well). Respect policies serve as reference points against which every questionable thought, word, and deed can be measured and judged. Every instance of harm between individuals lacks a measure of respect for the victim, including those that occur through the use of electronic devices.

Apart from their inclusion in policy manuals, respect policies should be disseminated within school materials to both students and parents and posted visibly in hallways and classrooms. While one might wish that students would automatically and naturally treat each other (and the adults in their lives) with respect, we know that in reality this does not always happen. As such, the respect policy reminds them of a standard that has been set and will be enforced.

It is also crucial that the school seeks to create and promote an environment where certain behaviors or language simply are not tolerated—by students and staff alike. In a school with a positive culture, students know what is appropriate and what is not. In these schools, there are a number of behaviors that the community as a whole would agree are simply "not cool." It isn't cool to bring a weapon to school. It isn't cool to get up in the middle of class and walk out of the classroom. It isn't cool to assault a teacher physically. It isn't cool to use racial slurs. Certain behaviors are simply not acceptable in the eyes of both adults and youth.

We hope that with education and effort, cyberbullying will someday be deemed "not cool." This ideal may be wishful thinking, but it is worth pursuing. All forms of bullying, no matter how minor, need to be condemned—with the responsible parties disciplined. If teachers deliberately ignore minor (or even serious) bullying because they just don't want to deal with it, what message does that send to the students? Students need to see that their teachers, counselors, and administrators take these behaviors seriously.

Periodical and Internet Sources Bibliography

The following articles have been selected to supplement the diverse views presented in this chapter.

Victoria Bekiempis — "What Makes Cyber-Bullying Laws Work?," *Village Voice*, May 22, 2012.

Michelle R. Davis — "Schools Tackle Legal Twists and Turns of Cyberbullying," *Education Week*, February 4, 2011.

Larry Edmonds — "Cyberbullying at Work: Some Never Grow Up," *Examiner*, May 10, 2012.

Education Insider — "Cyberbullying: A National Epidemic," October 6, 2010.

Tom Fox — "Bullying at Work," *Huffington Post*, May 1, 2012.

Matt Giffin — "Cyberbullying and the Tinker Standard," *Harvard Civil Rights–Civil Liberties Law Review*, October 17, 2011.

Jan Hoffman — "Online Bullies Pull Schools into the Fray" *New York Times*, June 27, 2010.

Avni Mehta — "The Law's Response to Cyberbullying," *The Champion*, May 2011.

Rick Nauert — "Social Workers Struggle to Deal with Cyber Bullying," Psych Central, January 11, 2011. http://psychcentral.com.

Dan Olweus — "Cyberbullying: An Overrated Phenomenon?," *European Journal of Developmental Psychology*, vol. 9, no. 5, 2012.

Jonathan Strickland — "Is Cyber Bullying Illegal?," DiscoveryNews, April 1, 2010. http://news.discovery.com.

CHAPTER 3

What Are the Etiquette and Ethics of Online Relationships?

Chapter Preface

For many, conducting a Google search on a prospective partner is a necessary part of preparing for a first date. Many commentators and experts have weighed in on this practice, discussing the wisdom and ethics of such investigations.

For example, Joanna Pearson writing in a September 12, 2008, article in the *New York Times* relates a story about how she had boasted to a potential date about her running. Later she went online and discovered that he ran competitively. When the two met again, she knew he was a faster runner than she was, and she was embarrassed that she had talked up her own ability. As a result, their conversation became awkward and painful. Pearson concludes that learning more about her date ruined the experience of getting to know him. "There's something to be said for the spontaneity and authentic facial expressions of utter ignorance," she argues.

Similarly, Anna Davies in a February 23, 2010, essay at The Frisky website says that she used to do extensive Google searches on all of her dates. Then, on one occasion, she discovered that her date had done an extensive Google search on *her*. In particular, he had found an embarrassing essay by her from several years earlier in which she had said that she preferred one-night stands to dating. She said:

> That was the lesson I needed. Going on a date with someone who had their own Internet-based idea of me—which was skewed and not really reflective of who I was as a real person—wasn't fun or enlightening. And I realized that in order to really get to know the guys I date, I need to stop searching and start connecting.

On the other hand, some people argue that Googling a date is reasonable and useful. In an August 2, 2005, article in the *Sacramento Bee,* Gina Kim interviewed a number of women who Googled dates to protect themselves. Jennifer Eidson said that Googling is "just a precaution. It's like carrying Mace. . . . To me, it's like a mini background check." Allegra Kim added, "It seems silly not to get a little bit of information if you can get it."

In a June 4, 2012, article on the Madame Noire website, Erika Ettin splits the difference between pro and con Googlers. She agrees that most people are going to find it hard to resist checking on a date but argues that Googlers should not let what they find prejudice them against their dates. "Try your hardest not to create a firm impression of this person in your mind before you meet," she said.

This chapter focuses on many issues of etiquette and ethics surrounding online dating and relationships.

> "Real, live online daters continue to find bizarre and almost impressively original ways to turn us off."

Good Netiquette Can Help Make Online Dating Work

Andrea Bartz and Brenna Ehrlich

Andrea Bartz is senior editor at Whole Living, *and Brenna Ehrlich is a senior writer/editor at MTV; both are netiquette columnists at CNN. In the following viewpoint, they argue that following good netiquette practices can help increase success in online dating. They say, for example, that refusing to put pictures on your dating profile, or refusing to share information, can be offputting, and that choosing a silly or self-deprecating username may also discourage potential dates. They conclude that a person who behaves thoughtfully online will have a better chance of attracting a partner.*

As you read, consider the following questions:

1. What do the authors say is the moral of the stories about approaching individuals from online dating sites off-line?

Andrea Bartz and Brenna Ehrlich, "Three Boneheaded Online Dating Moves to Avoid," CNN, February 15, 2012. Copyright © 2012 by Andrea Bartz and Brenna Ehrlich. All rights reserved. Reproduced by permission.

2. According to the authors, what is the effect when an online dating profile is left "totally unpopulated"?

3. What did a recent German study find about names displayed on online dating sites, according to the authors?

Ahh, yes, February 15, the joyful day when singletons can finally collapse in exhaustion after weeks of maintaining a nonchalant front. Finally, you think, finally, the incessant stream of hearts and Cupids and reminders that romantic partnership is the apogee of human achievement will come to a merciful end.

And then you voluntarily read to the second paragraph of our weekly netiquette column, silly! That's right, we're here to take you waist-deep into that cesspool of romantic endeavors and bad decisions: online dating.

Watching You on the Street

Because if you survived yesterday [that is, Valentine's Day] single, you might be gunning to circumvent a repeat performance in 2013 (i.e., another year of you listening to Alanis Morissette and sobbing softly in your bedroom or, conversely, having a faux-peppy who-needs-men night with your gal pals, swilling salmon-colored drinks and shooting hateful glances at the couples in the bar).

And if you're in a relationship right now, don't rest on your laurels quite yet: Breakups spike right after Cupid's big day, according to unofficial Facebook data, so you just might be back on the market soon.

We've told you what not to do with your first message to a prospective date. We've told you what not to do with your photo. Yet real, live online daters continue to find bizarre and almost impressively original ways to turn us off.

Read on for three totally boneheaded online dating moves we've actually encountered (AKA, weird things no one warns you about when they're persuading you to make a Match.com profile).

"Not to be creepy, but . . ." began an actual first message from an actual online dater. ". . . were you sitting on a bench at such-and-such intersection at about 6:15 last night? I'm not hitting on you, I just like to think of online dating as a city-wide game of Guess Who." Yes, we were at said corner, and we were unaware we were being watched by a peeper on the street.

The incredible thing is not that said dater recognized a human from the site—in an urban area, where folks are bumbling around in their own overlapping circles, of course you'll spot people whom you recognize from their profiles.

The key is to not acknowledge it in a creepy way. (A clue that you're not adhering to that guideline: You begin a message with, "Not to be creepy, but . . .")

In this instance, for example, if the dude wanted to go on a date, he could send a friendly first message (not mentioning the unwitting run-in). Then, if things were rolling along after a few dates, he could mention it in a fun, "You won't believe how serendipitous this was!" kind of way.

Or if he couldn't wait that long, he could send a cute Missed Connections–style message: "I think I walked by you in Union Square yesterday! Your purple peacoat was stunning. I see you're a big fan of *Parks & Recreation*—have you checked out *Party Down*?" But just announcing, apropos of nothing, that he has superior facial recognition skills? Kind of weird.

A friend told a tale of a girl he'd been messaging who eventually stopped responding. A few weeks later, a new note in his inbox: "Hey, were you at the Caveman concert last night?" (Indeed, he had been. Without the benefit of knowing a girl was watching him like Mel in *Flight of the Conchords*.) If she was loving his vibes in person, she certainly could have walked up to him in between sets and said hello. But since she'd already dropped the message volley like a hot potato, probably best to let sleeping dogs snore.

Another friend stopped messaging with a dude online when she got a weird feeling about him from his notes; a few weeks later, he spotted her at a Thai restaurant and marched right in. With apparent disregard for all social mores, he sat down at the table with her friends and asked when they could plan a proper date.

The recommended course of action here is obvious: Since she had already rejected him online, he should've respected that and let the girl and her friends finish their pad thai in peace.

Moral of these stories? Don't be scary. Online dating is nerve-racking enough when you're all squirmy-scared of rejection and awkward first-date conversations. Having to worry about weirdos jangling up to you at the supermarket? Not necessary. (Oh, and if you're the creep-ee: Block 'em on the site, or if they're approaching you in person, make an excuse and hightail it out of there. Safety first!)

Revealing Nothing About Yourself

It's a strange power play, leaving your profile free from pictures and with only the pithiest write-ups; it says, "You may need to advertise yourself like a heifer all gussied up for the state fair, but I ... I will make no attempt to sell myself to you. Instead," it tacitly blathers on, "I will decide whether you look interesting enough for me."

Maybe that works for some people (probably those seeking the weakest and most damaged goods). Our take: Having an online dating profile and leaving it totally unpopulated just makes you look like you have no good qualities to trumpet. Oh, and sending along a photo with your first message? Still silly. How come everyone else has to show their cards from the start, while you get to keep yours close to your chest? It reeks of insecurity, a gross, musky smell reminiscent of Axe body spray and tears.

Choosing a Stupid Username

A recent German study found that people with ugly names have less success on online dating sites. Researchers came to that conclusion by tracking profile views on a gloriously German-looking dating site where users go by their real first names.

But thank God you live in a country where you're free to pick your JDate handle!

So why, why, why would you pick something ugly (MoldyBill) or embarrassed sounding (JustBrowzin228)? There are so very many cards stacked against you in finding love (see: a montage of your February 14), so pick a simple username, write an honest profile, and pray to the good god Eros for better luck next year.

> "*Given the potentially serious conse-
> quences of intervening in people's ro-
> mantic lives, one could argue that the
> standards required of online dating
> sites' scientific investigations should be
> especially high.*"

There Is Little Evidence That Online Dating Works

Eli J. Finkel, Paul W. Eastwick, Benjamin R. Karney, Harry T. Reis, and Susan Sprecher

Eli J. Finkel is a professor at Northwestern University; Paul W. Eastwick is an assistant professor at Texas A&M University; Benjamin R. Karney is a professor at the University of California, Los Angeles; Harry T. Reis is a professor at the University of Rochester; and Susan Sprecher is a professor at Illinois State University; all work in the area of psychology. In the following viewpoint, they argue that there is little evidence that online dating algorithms or methods work effectively to match partners. They point out that there are no independent scientific studies of online dating algorithms and that the companies' claims for suc-

Adapted from: Eli J. Finkel, Paul W. Eastwick, Benjamin R. Karney, Harry T. Reis, and Susan Sprecher, "Online Dating: A Critical Analysis from the Perspective of Psychological Science," *Psychological Science in the Public Interest*, vol. 13, no. 1, January 2012, pp. 23–28. Copyright © 2012. Reproduced with permission of SAGE Publications, Inc. via Copyright Clearance Center.

cess could be explained by placebo effects or as the result of distorted samples. The authors conclude that the claims of online dating sites need to be held to higher standards.

As you read, consider the following questions:

1. What example do the authors provide of a news program uncritically parroting the claims of an online dating site?

2. According to the authors, what two standards must dating sites adhere to at minimum to show that their claims are scientifically valid?

3. How do the authors define confirmation bias, and how might it affect dating sites?

Perhaps not surprisingly, online dating sites' claims of superiority are pervasive. We briefly review the general thrust of these claims, offering a handful of concrete examples, before discussing the legal context for considering such claims and evaluating whether the evidence underlying them meets conventional standards of scientific validity.

Claims of Superiority

Online dating sites make a broad range of explicit and implicit claims about their access, communication, and matching services. ... Claims regarding access frequently involve information about how many people use the site and how useful the profiles are for learning about potential partners. Claims regarding communication frequently involve information about what forms of mediated communication the site offers and how these forms of communication are especially effective and efficient at helping users (a) develop a nuanced view of what potential partners are like and (b) discern whether those potential partners are likely to be compatible with them. Claims regarding matching frequently provide a broad-brushstroke analysis of how the site implements the matching process (e.g., personality matching, genetic matching) and why this means of implementation is likely to be effective.

News agencies frequently parrot these claims uncritically. They often do so in awed tones, presenting the coverage as news even though it sometimes more closely approximates an infomercial for the dating site. For example, *Good Morning America (GMA)*, ABC's popular morning television program, recently featured GenePartner, a dating site that claims to match potential partners based on their DNA. As part of this segment, *GMA* interviewed Tamara Brown, cofounder of GenePartner, who informed viewers that her company's system of establishing "biological compatibility" is "really, really accurate." Fortunately for her, *GMA*, with the ABC News logo featured prominently on the screen, was happy to spread the gospel, introducing the segment as follows: "Now, hard science is making it easier to find true love. A new matchmaking system uses DNA to help find your dream date, and it's redefining what it means to be compatible." *GMA* elaborated: "But making that first match has always been an inexact science, kissing a few frogs, unavoidable. Until now. With the use of DNA technology, the science of online dating has become a whole lot less inexact." Despite a paucity of evidence that DNA-based compatibility has an important influence on romantic outcomes, *GMA* functioned in this instance as a crucial component of GenePartner's public relations efforts. And, of course, *GMA* is not alone, and GenePartner is not the only dating site covered so effusively. Comparable segments pervade coverage of online dating across the news media, which makes it especially important for psychological scientists to provide a critical evaluation of dating sites' claims.

The Legal Context

Dating sites' claims do not exist in a vacuum. The online dating industry is part of the broader business world, and gov-

115

ernmental agencies have long regulated what sorts of claims businesses are allowed to make. Many dating sites, especially algorithm-based matching sites, claim that their methods have been scientifically demonstrated to yield positive romantic outcomes. Some sites, including Match.com and eHarmony, even report results from studies they have conducted or commissioned in support of their claims. However, these sites typically do not reveal the specifics of how their procedures work, especially vis-à-vis matching algorithms. As elaborated below, disclosure of these specifics is necessary for substantive evaluation of the validity of such claims. For example, the general claim that a dating site matches potential partners on the basis of the compatibility of their personality or values cannot be evaluated meaningfully because it omits information about which personality traits or values are considered and assessed, which are given greater or lesser weight, and how compatibility is established.

We recognize that these procedures, especially the matching algorithms, represent the proprietary intellectual property of their firms, who are understandably reluctant to reveal the formulae that make their services distinctive and possibly more effective relative to competitors. Secrecy of this sort is standard in the for-profit sector. The formula for Coca-Cola is famously clandestine, and Apple reveals the inner workings of its operating systems only to software developers who sign nondisclosure agreements. Nevertheless, firms like Coca-Cola and Apple rarely make explicit reference to a scientific basis for their marketing claims, perhaps in part because the Federal Trade Commission (FTC) Act

> prohibits unfair or deceptive advertising in any medium. . . . Advertising must tell the truth and not mislead consumers. . . . Claims must be substantiated, especially when they concern health, safety, or performance. . . . If your ad specifies a certain level of support for a claim— "tests show X"—you must have at least that level of support.

It may be instructive to draw an analogy to the pharmaceutical and medical-device industries, two other industries in which a product may have substantial implications for the health and well-being of its users. . . . These companies also assert that the benefits of their products are based on substantial scientific research. In fact, such evidence is a prerequisite for receiving approval from the U.S. Food and Drug Administration (FDA), consistent with this organization's responsibility to protect the public's welfare. Nevertheless, the sponsor of an investigative drug or device must submit detailed information about its chemical or mechanical properties and the underlying manufacturing process before being allowed to conduct a study on humans. Furthermore, although the FDA keeps certain proprietary information confidential, patent applications, which are public documents, must disclose key details. Thus, by the time a drug or device becomes available to the public, key information about its central components is accessible to scientists and other interested people. To our knowledge, no dating site has provided information of this sort to any regulatory agency.

Scientific Validity

These legal considerations notwithstanding, a crucial question is whether dating sites' claims are scientifically valid. An affirmative answer to this question depends, at minimum, upon the matching site (a) reporting the research methods and statistical analyses in sufficient detail to allow for independent replication and (b) adhering to consensually accepted standards for interpreting data as free from artifact [that is, an inaccurate observation or result]. To date, dating sites fall short on both of these necessary criteria.

Regarding the first criterion—reporting the research in sufficient detail to allow for independent replication—dating sites collect proprietary data and report whichever results they like in order to make claims about the propriety procedures

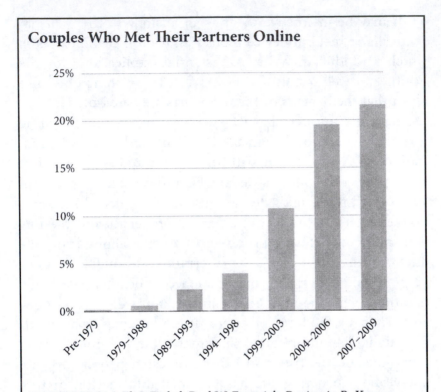

Couples Who Met Their Partners Online

TAKEN FROM: Eli J. Finkel, Paul W. Eastwick, Benjamin R. Karney, Harry T. Reis, and Susan Sprecher, "Online Dating: A Critical Analysis from the Perspective of Psychological Science," *Psychological Science in the Public Interest*, vol. 13, no. 1, January 2012, p. 13.

they use to introduce singles to one another. It is impossible for independent scholars to evaluate the validity of a given matching algorithm because the matching sites refuse to share the algorithm with members of the scientific community. Such open sharing is standard in science.

A related issue is that online dating sites rarely publish their empirical findings in peer-reviewed reports. Indeed, we found no published, peer-reviewed papers—or Internet postings, for that matter—that explained in sufficient detail (that is, sufficient to allow determination of whether the data are free from artifact or sufficient to permit replication) the criteria used by dating sites for matching or for selecting which profiles a user gets to peruse. Scientific journals generally require this kind of information to evaluate a paper for publication. . . .

Since at least 2004, scholars have repeatedly noted the necessity of dating sites providing fully documented scientific studies to support their various claims, but the sites have not adhered to these standards. Until the science underlying the purported effectiveness of online dating protocols is subjected to the standard scrutiny, scientific claims regarding the construction or effectiveness of such protocols should be given little credence.

Regarding the second criterion—adherence to consensually accepted standards for interpreting data as free from artifact—the empirical reports from online dating sites fall well short of accepted standards for establishing that any effects they might find are due to the mechanisms they claim. For example, even if a dating site shared sufficient information for scholars to be confident that couples formed through that site were more satisfied than were couples formed through other means, the site would also have to show that any such differences were due to the sites' procedures rather than to a broad range of potential confounds in the research. All dating sites function as dating interventions, and there is a long tradition in the behavioral and medical sciences of evaluating the impact of interventions. We discuss three issues in the online dating literature—selection bias, expectancy effects, and the need for randomized experiments—that converge upon the conclusion that the evidence dating sites have reported to date is susceptible to troubling artifacts.

i. Selection bias. Published research comparing couples who met through a given dating site to those who met through some other means are compromised by *selection bias*, which refers to a statistical artifact in which conclusions are distorted by the existence of systematic differences between groups that are unrelated to any variable the researchers are investigating. For example, when eHarmony scholars reported that couples who had met through eHarmony exhibited stronger marital adjustment than couples who had met through "unfettered selection," they failed to rule out a broad range of plausible differences between the people in these two groups that caused half of them to join eHarmony in the first place. People who seek to establish a romantic relationship online are not a random sample of single people who are unattached and interested in a relationship; instead, and minimally, they tend to be people who are highly motivated to establish a romantic relationship. Such motivation may cause these people to evaluate with favoritism any company that offers access to a large pool of potential partners or to be more likely to commit to a relationship. In addition, people with the financial resources and social-psychological skills to join a dating site (especially eHarmony) and to pass the background screening implemented by some sites (especially eHarmony) may be better candidates for successful relationships than other people.

ii. Expectancy effects. A second issue plaguing research comparing couples who met through a given dating site to those who met through some other means pertains to the possibility of *expectancy effects,* which refer to the myriad ways that research participants' expectancies can bias a study's results. In particular, it seems plausible that users of a given matching site have some degree of faith in the matching algorithm's validity, and we suggest that this faith can cause them to experience positive romantic outcomes, at least in the short term, that are entirely unrelated to the content of the algorithm. Scholars have identified at least three interrelated processes that may lend indirect support for this proposition.

One process, which resides at the intersection of research on *outcome dependency* and research on the *endowment effect* and the *status quo bias,* begins with the recognition that assigning users an algorithm-selected match causes them to perceive that they have progressed through several early stages of the dating process, including narrowing the field of potential partners and finding somebody with whom they might be especially compatible. Given various pieces of evidence that the perception that one has progressed through the early stages of a given process increases one's motivation to continue with that process, a user of a dating site may be especially motivated to pursue a relationship with an algorithm-identified match.

A second process that may emerge as a result of users' faith in the validity of a site's algorithm is the *placebo effect*, which refers to improvements in one's psychological or physical well-being, or in one's satisfaction with a particular experience, that result from the erroneous belief that one has received an efficacious intervention. A user's belief in the validity of the algorithm used by a dating site may cause him or her to view a match as compatible. That is, having a purportedly authoritative source claim to use science to select putatively ideal or highly compatible matches could predispose people to be more accepting of these matches, at least initially, than they might otherwise be. Such a belief may increase their likelihood of contacting, and perhaps experiencing initial attraction toward, him or her.

The third process is the *confirmation bias*, which refers to the tendency for people to seek or interpret evidence in ways that are likely to support their existing beliefs or expectations. Whereas the placebo effect may cause users of matching sites to behave in accord with the belief that selected potential partners are in fact compatible with them, the confirmation bias may help sustain this belief, at least in the short term, by inspiring hypothesis tests that are systematically biased toward confirming it. For example, a user might pursue certain lines of conversation with a selected potential partner that are especially likely to provide evidence of compatibility (e.g., discussing known common interests rather than more ambiguous topics).

iii. The need for randomized experiments. Selection bias and expectancy effects are troubling methodological artifacts, but scholars can overcome them by employing optimal research designs. Most researchers believe that randomized trials, in which participants are randomly assigned either to an intervention condition or to one or more suitable control conditions, are the gold standard for evaluating the effectiveness of an intervention. Random assignment is crucial because it rules out various threats to internal validity. Unfortunately, our extensive literature review revealed no randomized experiments evaluating the effectiveness of dating sites or of the matching procedures that these sites use.

Unconvincing Claims of Superiority

In sum, online dating sites frequently claim that people will achieve better romantic outcomes when seeking partners through their sites than through conventional off-line dating (or through other dating sites). Such claims have been trumpeted by news organizations that frequently celebrate dating sites' services without providing sufficient critical analysis, and regulatory agencies have, it seems, adopted a laissez-faire attitude toward these claims. Our investigation suggests, however, that dating sites have failed to provide any compelling evidence for these claims. As such, the claims simply cannot be accepted as valid.

The severe limitations of dating sites' scientific reports are especially disconcerting when they are compared to the rigorous scientific standards for reporting research in other areas that have immediate relevance to the public welfare. For example, according to the author guidelines of the *Journal of the American Medical Association* (JAMA), all articles must include at least one named author who is independent of any commercial funder or sponsor and who indicates that she or he "had full access to all the data in the study and takes responsibility for the integrity of the data and the accuracy of the data analysis." Furthermore,

> for industry-sponsored studies, an analysis of the data (based on the entire raw data set and evaluation of the study protocol and a prespecified plan for data analysis) must be conducted by an independent statistician at an academic institution rather than by statisticians employed by the sponsor or by a commercial contract research organization.... The results of this independent statistical analysis should be the results reported in the manuscript.

Given the potentially serious consequences of intervening in people's romantic lives, one could argue that the standards required of online dating sites' scientific investigations should be especially high. It is unfortunate that they have been, to date, especially low.

> "Do not tell me that sending naked photos of myself is dangerous. Because sure, he could show it to his friends, but so what? I look great."

Adult Sexting Is Fun and Harmless

Penelope Trunk

Penelope Trunk is a writer, blogger, and career advisor, as well as the founder of the Brazen Careerist *blog. In the following viewpoint, she discusses her dating life after her divorce and says one of the men she dated asked her to send a naked photo of herself. She says she is unconcerned about the man she is dating sharing the photo with others, first because she looks good in the photo, and second because adults regularly send such pictures; it is common and accepted, Trunk claims. She concludes that sexting is fun and harmless for adults.*

As you read, consider the following questions:

1. How does Trunk say that her Asperger syndrome affects her?

Penelope Trunk, "The Joys of Adult Sexting," *Newsweek/Daily Beast*, June 6, 2011. Copyright © 2011 The Newsweek/Daily Beast Company LLC. All rights reserved. Used by permission and protected by the Copyright Laws of the United States. The printing, copying, redistribution, or retransmission of the Material without express written permission is prohibited.

2. Why does Trunk call herself the Ansel Adams of nude self-portraits?

3. How does Trunk say she knows that sending nude photos is not that big a deal?

Three years ago I divorced with no clue as to how people date. I think I probably never had a clue about how people date, because I have Asperger syndrome. This mental deficit means that I am bad at understanding social rules, since most are not written down. And I'm bad at understanding nonverbal communication, which is basically 100 percent of the real communication of dating.

I am very easy to get into bed because the dance people do before getting to the sex part does not make sense to me. Here's a post where I describe what it's like to have sex with me. But here's the bottom line: Once I'm there, clothes off, I'm a lot of trouble. Because there is not really a way to get from clothes off to bodies connected without a sort of nonverbal dance of pleasure. Or displeasure. Or something.

So I decided that I have two things going for me: I am usually the smartest woman a guy has ever dated. This gets me through the terrible conversations. The guy thinks to himself that he knows I'm not stupid, so maybe he is stupid and that's why I sound stupid. Really. This is what I think they think.

The other thing I have going for me is that I have a great body. I used to play professional beach volleyball. Sponsors paid to put their name on my butt. I signed autographs in a bikini. So each time a guy thinks that I'm too much of a whack-job to put up with, he remembers how hot I am, and he keeps going.

The problem is that 15 years and one divorce later, I was not sure I had the body to pull off that delicate balancing act. I worried that as I get older, I get more quirky and more saggy, and it's a bad combination for dating.

I did a lot of research about breast lifts and tummy tucks, while I wondered, can you date a guy if the first time he sees you is when you have post-breast-feeding breasts. What if he's never even seen that? It's not fair. I want breast implants.

That's what I told myself. And, as you know, divorce is a tough time, and I was able to pretty much distract myself by obsessing over the sagginess of my breasts. And, also, is it fair to wear a push-up bra? Is it misrepresentation? These are things I had to find out.

In the meantime, I have a very popular blog. And as soon as I announced I was getting a divorce, my blog became my personal dating site.

One fun story is the 25-year-old. He himself is not that interesting. In fact, if you are in your forties and you date a 25-year-old, it's safe to say that the kid is going to bore you to death, but it sure was fun to try that out. I'm not going to tell you about all guys. Although the alcoholic who had the same divorce lawyer that I did appears to still be available and he's very rich, so maybe you should read about him if you're looking for that type.

The guy I do want to tell you about is the one who lived five states away. We texted all the time. This created many moral dilemmas, such as, can I text about a blow job while I'm eating McFlurries with my kids. (Answer: Yes)

One night I was at the gym, and I was naked, getting ready to shower, when a woman in my aisle said to me, "Are you Penelope Trunk?"

I knew it was going to be bad. I reached for a towel to cover myself, realized I forgot to bring one, and then said, "Yes."

She said, "I love your book so much. I wish I had it here for you to sign. Can you sign a piece of paper?"

Insane request, yes. But it's hard to think fast when you are naked. So I signed the paper. Then I told the guy I was dating. He said, "The story would be so much better with a photo. Send me one."

I laughed.

He did not laugh.

I said, "Naked?"

Of course, he said yes.

He said, "Do it now," like he is a 15-year-old fixated on getting his hands on his first piece of porn. Or like he is Mickey Rourke in *9½ Weeks*. Not that I saw the movie. But I read the book and the surrounding literary criticism so I could understand the dynamics of men giving orders to women.

Sort of hot. If you let the guy do it.

So I went to the back of the showers, and I laid down in a dressing room because if you lay down you look thin. I clicked. But then my breasts sort of flopped to each side.

I spent an hour taking photos. I moved dressing rooms. I tried standing in the shower without the water on. I remember reading that Ansel Adams took 1,000 shots for each masterpiece we know today. I think I'm the Ansel Adams of nude self-portraits. After 1,000 tries, I had a masterpiece. Perfect lighting so that nothing looked fat, perfect camera angle for smooth skin and fluffy breasts, and perfect timing because he surely thought I would never send the photo, so it was like a surprise in the mail.

Do not tell me that sending naked photos of myself is dangerous. Because sure, he could show it to his friends, but so what? I look great. I hope he can get the photo in *Maxim* because I might never look that good again in my whole life.

And what will his friends think of me? Probably nothing. Because they have women sending nude photos of themselves. It's not that big a deal. You know how I know? Because the state of Vermont (and other states as well) is trying to pass a law that decriminalizes sending nude photos of oneself if you are underage. That's right: For years, even though kids were

The War on Sex

Sexting [sending sexually explicit messages or images by cell phone] started spontaneously between owners of the powerful new generation of mobile phones, who suddenly had high-quality cameras with them every day—which needed no film, and therefore no film processing by nosy strangers. Like adults, minors started taking sexy pictures of themselves or each other, sending them to boyfriends, girlfriends, or groups of people. Law enforcement officials across the country immediately labeled this activity as distribution of child porn, and threatened that those who were caught would be arrested and even jailed—which is exactly what happened.

Despite predictions that sexting will invite sexual assault and ruin lives, no one has proven that sexting does any real harm. Ten years from now, everyone applying to Harvard Medical School or Stanford Law School will have nude pictures of themselves on the Internet, and perspective employers of these young people will just shrug. It's similar to tattoos 15 years ago—people predicted that those getting inked would regret their indelible choice as they lost out on jobs (and quality mates). Now you can't find a gynecologist or CPA [certified public accountant] without one.

The real issue with sexting is the regulation of teen sexuality. The War on Sex—already withholding medical and contraceptive information and supplies from teens, already criminalizing a wide range of teen sexual behaviors—has now organized this latest attempt to colonize the bodies of America's teens.

Marty Klein, America's War on Sex: The Attack on Law, Lust, and Liberty. *Santa Barbara, CA: ABC-CLIO, 2012, p. 122.*

sending nude photos of themselves to someone they wanted to show it to, the act was illegal—an act of trafficking in child pornography.

But sending nude photos is so common today that law-makers are forced to treat it as a mainstream courting ritual and legalize it for all ages.

Sending a naked photo of yourself is an emotionally inti-mate act because of the implied trust you have in the recipi-ent. When you act in a trusting way—like trusting the recipi-ent of the photo to handle it with care and respect—you benefit because being a generally trusting person is an emo-tionally sound thing to do; people who are trusting are better judges of character. This is because people who are trusting get burned a lot and learn from that. People who are suspi-cious all the time won't learn nearly as quickly who is trust-worthy, according to research reported in *Psychology Today*.

Also, if you're worried about your career, you can relax. Anthony Weiner, the most comically animated, intellectually captivating, Internet-ready member of Congress, just tweeted an alleged photo of himself in underwear. Or not. Actually, it was not really his whole self, just the what's-covered-by-underwear self. But his constituents don't care.

But here's some good news: As long as you make yourself look hot in the photo, you'll probably be okay. Because good-looking people earn more money, have more friends, and have more fun in life than the not-good-looking. So if you can fig-ure out how to take a good photo of yourself, text it to any-one you want. And if you want to know how to send the photo via Twitter, ask Congressman Weiner for some tips.

> "Commanders can use text messages and photos as evidence to prove an extra-marital affair or other behavior deemed counter to good order and discipline."

Adult Sexting Can Destroy Careers and Relationships

Joe Gould and Gina Cavallaro

Joe Gould and Gina Cavallaro are staff writers at Army Times. *In the following viewpoint, they report that sending and receiving sexual text messages, or sexting, can ruin careers, especially in the military. The reporters say that sexually explicit text messages often provide evidence of infidelity and poor judgment that can result in expulsion from the army or loss of rank. They say that this problem has been exacerbated as cell phones have proliferated even among soldiers deployed overseas. The writers also say that the ease of sexting can fuel sex addiction, destroying marriages and careers.*

As you read, consider the following questions:

1. What do the authors say is the army's official policy on sexting?

Joe Gould and Gina Cavallaro, "Explicit Messages, Images Put Careers at Risk," *Armed Forces Journal*, October 10, 2011. Copyright © 2011 Gannett. All rights reserved. Used by permission and protected by the Copyright Laws of the United States. The printing, copying, redistribution, or retransmission of the Material without express written permission is prohibited.

2. Why do people engage in sexting, according to behavioral health experts?

3. How does Michael Leahy describe the relationship between sexting and sex addiction?

It began with some flirtatious text messages between an advanced individual training instructor and a young female trainee, and it quickly turned physical. The illicit relationship between the staff sergeant, who was almost 40, and the 19-year-old student was their secret, but not for long.

Sexting Can Hurt Soldiers

When the young woman, after running into some minor disciplinary trouble, turned in the instructor, the text messages between the two were used as proof of the relationship, and it was the instructor whose career was over.

With growing frequency, soldiers are using cell phones and other digital media to swap sexually explicit images and messages as they conduct relationships—adulterous, underage, violations of fraternization policies, or otherwise inappropriate—that the Army frowns on. Sexting has severed marriages, ended careers and landed some soldiers in jail.

Sexting—the sharing of explicit images and messages via cell phone and other digital media—has made headlines over scandals at civilian schools and driven some states to contemplate legislation.

The Army has no specific policy on sexting. Nor does it maintain data on incidents in which soldiers are investigated or disciplined for sexting. But attorneys who specialize in military justice say they have seen a spike in inquiries from service members accused of crimes or violations stemming from it. And the digital evidence left behind is frequently undeniable—and usually ruinous.

"In all these sex cases today, they're sending each other pictures," said Patrick McLain, a retired major and court-martial trial judge with a civilian law practice in Dallas. His caseload involving sexting-related infractions is up noticeably over the last two years, he said. Soldiers and other troops who contact him are often trying to determine whether it's worth paying for legal representation when the evidence against them is so damning.

Among consenting adult soldiers and civilians, sexting is legal, provided they are not exchanging lewd images of minors. Sexting among soldiers is legal as well, according to attorneys who specialize in military cases. Unlike in the civilian world, however, where compromising photos or messages might be scandalous, those same pictures and texts can cost soldiers their careers because the activity that's connected to them may constitute fraternization or inappropriate behavior.

Many single service members and couples embrace discreet sexting as a means to maintain a romantic connection through long deployments and other times of extended separation. Others do it to cheat. And the service has a history of coming down hard on illicit activity and poor judgment.

"I would say the majority of sex offenses and adultery these days involve some form of text messages," said attorney Greg Rinckey, a former Army judge advocate general and managing partner of the law firm Tully Rinckey PLLC. "For almost every officer or enlisted who consults me about adultery, there are text messages."

Observers say the military has no special monopoly on illicit sexual contact of this sort. Former New York congressman Anthony Weiner, who is married, resigned his seat in scandal earlier this year [in 2011] after racy cell phone photos he sent to young women via Twitter became public.

The apparent surge in illicit sexual activity among service members appears to have followed the proliferation of smartphones and Internet access downrange [that is, on overseas deployment], said Jerry Powell, director of the Fayetteville Family Life Center, a faith-based counseling center near Fort Bragg, N.C.

When Powell, a former Army chaplain, was in Iraq in 2005, it was "not common at all" for deployed soldiers to have cell phones, nor was this an issue.

"Everything has changed; the Internet was not that easy to access," he said. "Now no matter what your rank, everybody has a cell phone, and it has instant e-mail and web access."

Getting in Trouble

While there's no specific mention of sexting in the Uniform Code of Military Justice [UCMJ], sexting is often accompanied by activities that are covered in the UCMJ. Commanders can use text messages and photos as evidence to prove an extramarital affair or other behavior deemed counter to good order and discipline. Moreover, unsolicited sexting has been highlighted in some sexual assault complaints.

"We see it a lot," said Grover Baxley, a defense attorney who specializes in military law. "In any rape case, you're going to see investigators, or the defense, go and say, 'Hey, can we find any contact between these two individuals either before the alleged act occurred, or even after?' For example, if we can find friendly text messages going back and forth between the complainant and the accused after an alleged nonconsensual act, that's relevant information."

Sexting, in other words, provides evidence that old-fashioned, hardwired phone calls didn't provide—particularly in military cases.

"Five years ago, before texting became so frequent," he said, "we didn't have this ability to retrieve the actual content of conversations. Now, what were formerly 'he said, she said' cases become cases where definitive proof is available."

In July, Lt. Col. Lonnie McNair, commander of the Raleigh Recruiting Battalion in North Carolina, was suspended after a sergeant in the unit accused McNair of having an affair with his wife. A forensic exam of the wife's phone, paid for by the sergeant, revealed that McNair and the wife exchanged text messages to arrange liaisons, trade sexual talk and share photos.

The sergeant accused McNair of sending a picture of his genitals to the sergeant's wife. McNair refused to comment on the allegations.

In 2008 at Fort Leonard Wood, Mo., a dozen drill sergeants and trainers were punished for having forbidden sexual contact with female trainees. According to published reports, the women in many cases initiated the relationship, often through text messages or social networking sites.

A staff sergeant with 577th Engineer Battalion had sex with a trainee and later tried to get her to delete text messages between them and to deny the relationship. He was sentenced to a reduction in rank to E-3 and five months' confinement.

In April, a Texas woman came forward to accuse a 35-year-old Army recruiter who visited her high school in 2009 of sexually assaulting her and later sending her sexually explicit text messages for weeks.

In 2009, a 27-year-old private from Fort Campbell, Ky., was arrested in the company of a 15-year-old girl and accused of sending her text messages expressing his intent to impregnate her.

According to published reports, he allegedly instructed another underage girl to send him a picture of her genital area, which she did.

Some observers note the popularity of texting, coupled with the ease of using a cell phone's camera and the ability to instantly transmit images, has ushered in an era in which people take a more casual view of once carefully calculated efforts to conceal sexually explicit behavior.

The consequences of having images and compromising messages fall into the wrong hands can cause trouble for any service member, said Jack Zimmermann, a retired Marine prosecutor and criminal trial judge based in Houston.

But for officers, held to a higher standard, the fallout can be especially severe.

"Who would intentionally and willingly snap a photo of themselves by any means knowing that people who work for those officers would see it?" said Zimmermann, a retired Marine colonel. "It could detract from those officers' authority. It could easily be construed as being such poor judgment that it's conduct unbecoming."

The temptation for sexting can be hard to resist. People engage in sexting because it's easy and instantaneously gratifying, according to behavioral health experts.

Sexting and Sexual Addiction

Sexting is addictive, and a gateway to more destructive behavior, according to Michael Leahy, a self-described recovering sex addict, inspirational speaker and author of five sex books, including *Porn Nation*.

"Sexting is the crack cocaine of sexual addiction," Leahy said.

Leahy said he has counseled several men whose marriages were on the rocks because of the men's escalating need for more. Leahy's 15-year marriage collapsed because of his insatiable need to find sex any way he could, he said.

The behavior that fuels sex addiction is a big problem in the military, he said, especially for troops downrange.

"You start as a recreational user, couple hours a week, and in a high-pressure environment, it's not unreasonable. But what happens when that becomes a couple of hours a day? One of the forms of escalation is going from looking at pictures to voyeurism or exhibition like . . . peeping or exposing yourself," he said. "It's a heightened sexual experience."

Leahy and his second wife, an active-duty Army sergeant, have helped troops overcome sex addiction through a faith-based program, and they have provided counseling materials to deployed military behavioral health specialists.

But those specialists, while acknowledging there is a problem, say few sex addicts come forward.

"I have only been approached one time in the last six months regarding porn addiction, and the soldier never followed through," said an Army behavioral health specialist working downrange who asked not to be identified. "I think the overall mentality of your average soldier prevents even those that realize they have a problem and want help with it from actually seeking it."

And the behavior is hard to stop upon redeployment. Unlike watching porn on a computer or getting it in an e-mail, the instantaneous nature of sexting on a smartphone means soldiers can get a quick fix by looking at a picture they may have just received. Addiction, and a loss of intimacy with a spouse or significant other, may not be far behind.

"Sex addicts don't have relationships, they have serial sex acts with parts of other people's bodies," said Dr. [A.J.] Reid Finlayson, a practicing psychiatrist and sex addiction specialist at Vanderbilt University. "It can be compulsive."

Yale University military justice scholar Eugene Fidell said wireless technology has raised the stakes.

"It is such that with a few keystrokes, something like this can reach thousands of people and inflict great pain on the victim," he said.

Digital Lipstick

For married soldiers, digital lipstick on the collar can have just as devastating an effect as the real thing, said Powell, the counselor and former chaplain in Fayetteville.

"The great majority I've seen, one partner finds out about the affair by checking the cell phone logs, or by getting a password and checking e-mail accounts," he said.

Powell said one Army wife he is treating did not suspect her husband at all, but idly checked his cell phone one evening and discovered calls and text messages between him and another woman. It all began while the soldier was deployed.

"Lots of minutes, many times a day, and that's when it all broke," Powell said. "She was devastated."

Just as service members live on the edge at work, they can "walk on the edge emotionally" by engaging in forbidden relationships online.

"When you're downrange and you're dirty and you're tired and you're hungry, and you're looking for that emotional edge, it's very easy to find on the Internet," Powell said.

> "Being drawn into a cyber affair can be as destructive to a marriage as a physical affair."

Cybersex Affairs Are a Form of Infidelity

Lenore Skomal

Lenore Skomal is a public speaker and author; she also teaches journalism at schools including Gannon University. In the following viewpoint, she reports that it is becoming easier for people to engage in cybersex or relationships online. She says that such relationships often seem as if they are not really infidelity, since there is often no personal contact. However, she argues, cyber relationships involve lying and emotional commitment, and they can destroy a marriage just as easily as physical infidelity can.

As you read, consider the following questions:

1. What does Tina B. Tessina say makes cybersex easier over traditional affairs?

2. What is unconscious misrepresentation, according to LeslieBeth Wish?

Lenore Skomal, "Infidelity: Online Affairs Are Fantasy for Cheating Spouses, Can Lead to Divorce," Divorce360.com, 2009. Copyright © 2009 by Lenore Skomal. All rights reserved. Reproduced by permission.

3. According to the viewpoint, when is the precise moment when someone is cheating in a cybersex relationship?

Psychologists call it the final frontier. It's cybersex, and it has become the easiest way to cheat on your spouse. "Thirty years ago it was much harder to get sex. You had to sneak around and really look for it. Cybersex brings it right into the house. It is just so easy now," said Tina B. Tessina, 64, a Long Beach, Calif.-based psychotherapist and author of *Money, Sex and Kids: Stop Fighting About the Three Things That Can Ruin Your Marriage* (Adams Media 2008). "Cybersex is also easier to hide and it usually doesn't cost money."

Cybersex Comes of Age

With cyberspace's coming of age so have multiple opportunities to meet someone online and get romantically involved. Chat rooms, interactive websites, blogging and public networking forums like Myspace and Facebook have inadvertently invited strangers into many bedrooms. In fact, the Internet hookup has become so commonplace, it's now considered as viable as any other venue to meet someone.

"I suppose it's as good as a bar," said Alice Aspen March, Los Angeles–based author of *The Attention Factor* [blog]. "The only difference is at a bar you actually see and talk to a person in the flesh. When you go on the Internet, you are getting a connection with a person in the machine. And it's really a fantasy to have an affair on a machine. It is not real."

That aspect [of] fantasy might be why so many married people get lured into affairs online when that was not their original intent. "You could enter it innocently, not really looking for an affair. But it's very seductive so even a little curiosity can get you hooked. While the fantasy aspect is alluring, it can also lead to misrepresentation even without intent," said LeslieBeth Wish, 60, a psychologist and social worker based in Sarasota, Fla., who has been counseling couples in relationships for over 30 years.

The introduction of the Internet, she added, has changed the face of what had been the traditional affair. Namely, a sexual relationship between two people that happens in person with an element of physicality. The absence of that, she said, somehow allows for a big degree of denial about the relationship even being an affair in the first place.

Online affairs represent safety, fantasy and that big escape tunnel. They don't count because there is no one-to-one contact. Because they are viewed as a so-called emotional time-out. It's like the guys who go online for pornography. The Internet has created a powerful outlet for an already existing problem. People think it's safer. It's very easy to fool yourself by fooling your spouse. "Honey, it's not like I am meeting him. It's only online. What is the big deal?" Wish said.

Fantasy and Seduction

Boredom, curiosity and lack of communication with a spouse—all these have been blamed for online affairs blooming in the first place. While some argue how you get to investigating online sex options is important, others point to what happens once you get there as being what matters. It can create a real problem in your relationship at home.

"If a man is curious about threesomes, for instance, and doesn't talk to his wife about it because he thinks she wouldn't handle it well, he goes on one of the alternative sex sites where he will find a chat room that is free or low fee. In his mind, this is a safe, cheap alternative. He doesn't know these people. He will never meet them. And there he can connect up with people and talk about his fantasies," [says] Tessina. "But pretty soon, he finds someone he really connects with and off they go from the group on their own. It just moves like that."

The fact that there is never an actual meeting between the two and no face-to-face connection naturally lays the proving

Was It Sex?

Consider these two scenarios:

(1) Your beloved has moved overseas. To maintain your erotic relationship, you arrange to don virtual reality suits. . . .

One night, you agree to go all the way in virtual reality sex. Afterward, you are exhilarated but confused: Are you still virgins? You had vowed to give yourself to your one true love: Have you now consummated your relationship?

(2) You surprise your spouse at the computer, who is typing feverishly and breathing heavily. . . . You feel upset and betrayed, but have you been sexually betrayed? Is your spouse an adulterer?

Even, when we have filled in the details in each of these scenarios—the disposition of body parts and technical devices, the beliefs and desires of those involved—a residual confusion remains. Clearly something was going on in each case, but was it sex?

Louise Collins, "Is Cybersex Sex?,"
in The Philosophy of Sex: Contemporary Readings, *5th ed.*
Eds. Alan Soble and Nicholas Power.
Lanham, MD: Rowman & Littlefield, 2008, pp. 117–118.

ground for fantasy and even lies. What you see is not necessarily what you are getting, Wish said.

"People misrepresent themselves more online because they can. And sometimes they misrepresent themselves without knowing it. It's called 'unconscious misrepresentation.' They actually do believe they look like Robert Redford. Think of the people who try out for *American Idol*. They really believe they have talent, and they clearly don't. People have a lot of trouble assessing their own abilities and appearance. That is why we are so prone to flattery," she said.

"The online thing is really pure fantasy. You are fleshing out whatever skeleton they are giving you. Fleshing it out from your own imagination," Tessina said. "You don't think of it as lying. We all want to be liked. We have a tendency—even the most honest of us—still have a tendency to play up the things that other people respond to. It's human nature, and that gets exaggerated in this thing when your ego is at stake. You have a tendency to respond to this other person in whatever way they are reacting to and a lot of dishonesty starts happening."

"Most people don't set out to be dishonest. They don't set out to cheat on their spouses, but they get caught up in it, they are not emotionally mature enough to have the self-control to see it and to stop it," she added.

As was the case for Rich Mullikin from Galveston, Texas. "I was involved in an online affair for about 18 months which culminated in me buying a plane ticket to see the woman," wrote the 39-year-old public relations consultant in an e-mail interview. "I am married, and she was married. We chatted off and on for many months, but then it progressed faster and faster, sharing personal feelings, then sharing sexual fantasies."

In Mullikin's case, he didn't want an affair, but "little things snowball so fast" which the experts say is typical in a virtual affair. "Pretty soon, you go from being online for 20 minutes a day, then to an hour," said Wish. "It becomes addicting, and then you are staying up till until 2 a.m. or 3 a.m. online. It becomes like your virtual friend. And the problem is, that creates a level of emotional distance in your marriage, whether you acknowledge it or not."

And just like an addiction, "it rewards you every time," she said. "You feel good each time you talk to this person online. It reinforces itself." Which is precisely what makes it so very dangerous, added Tessina. "It's a very seductive thing. But if you have your priorities straight, you are not going to fall for it. It's just like drugs. People can try cocaine and not become cocaine addicts," she said. "As I often hear in counseling, clients will say, 'I had to stop. I liked it too much.' A warning will come up. People who have the emotional maturity to stop doing what they are doing are usually fine. It's the ones who don't know how to self-regulate. They can be sucked right into it."

Cyber Affairs

And being drawn into a cyber affair can be as destructive to a marriage as a physical affair, she added. "If anything, it is taking something away from your marriage," she said. "First, there is a kind of neglect. Neglect in terms of what you could be doing with your spouse and are not. And then lying, because you are not talking to your spouse about what is going on.

"And then that moves into cheating. When is the precise moment when you are actually cheating? When you feel like you are transferring your affection. And it doesn't have be physical."

For Mullikin, it never became physical. He never acted on his sexual fantasies with his cyber mistress, and wrote that his online trysts were a case of "the grass is always greener." But it was addictive. "I was addicted to the rush I felt when I chatted with her and spoke to her on the phone and even when I texted her back and forth. It was a high that felt good, made me feel invincible, and more like a man," he wrote.

When his wife found his e-mails, he came clean and told her the truth. But the road back to a functional marriage isn't easy. "Virtual relationships are real relationships that involve emotional bonding, and can drastically damage a marriage as much as a real affair," Tessina said. "The biggest problem is the betrayal of trust which takes a long time to rebuild. But it can be done."

Which was the case for Mullikin, who showed it indeed can be done. "Lots of counseling, attending a sex addicts program for about a year, and much self-reflection," he wrote. "I'm luckily still together with my wife who is my perfect soul mate. I'm in love more than ever with my wife who chose to give me a second chance. That's not a road I'll ever go down again."

> "Not everyone is going to be wigged out by a little online canoodling. Some might think it's kinda hot."

Cybersex Is Not Necessarily Infidelity

Violet Blue

Violet Blue is a blogger and writer whose work appears in outlets including Forbes.com and O, The Oprah Magazine. In the following viewpoint, she argues that cybersex can be a betrayal of a relationship in some situations, but it does not have to be. She points to couples who have relationships in which both partners participate in cybersex with others with the knowledge of the other partner. She suggests that the important thing is to be honest and to communicate with one's partner. She concludes that in some cases cybersex, even with other people, can be part of a couple's sex life rather than a betrayal of it.

As you read, consider the following questions:

1. Under what circumstances does Keely Kolmes say that cybersex may be real sex?

2. What signs might tell you that you are crossing the line into infidelity with cybersex, according to the viewpoint?

Violet Blue, "Is Cybersex Cheating?," SFGate.com, July 17, 2008. Copyright © 2008 by Violet Blue. All rights reserved. Reproduced by permission.

3. What does Ellie Lumpesse say about jealousy?

"Hey. Baby. I know you like to have some fun. You. Know. Where to find me," burbles Kari, the Virtual Girlfriend in a halting, female Stephen Hawking voice through my G4's speakers. But while Kari might be the most advanced commercially available artificial intelligence pleasure model online, if I walked in on a boyfriend having an 8-bit roll in the hay with her, I'd be fighting the urge to laugh, not the urge to throw dishes. Cybersex, it seems, might just be in the eye of the beholder.

Cybersex and Secrets

Right now there are more ways to have cybersex than ever thought possible, and it's making modern couples reconfigure their relationships' Terms of Service [ToS]. Cybersex makes it easy to cheat; you don't have to meet anyone, so the risk factor is low on all fronts—except maybe emotionally. Cybersex is also a more creative form of masturbation, so in many ways it's not too terribly different than enjoying porn or fantasy. But that cybersex often involves another human gives it a twist; walking in on a boyfriend with an actual human female on the other side of the screen, having a hot and heavy text or cam session—I don't need to consult our ToS to know that wouldn't feel good, at all.

But if it's really just masturbation, then is cybersex "real" sex? Dr. Keely Kolmes, Psy.D., a San Francisco psychotherapist for individuals and couples, tells me, "I would say that whether or not it is 'real' sex depends upon how the interaction is experienced by the participants. It may even feel 'real' for one person in the encounter, and not for the other person with whom they are having cybersex. On the other hand, you may have two people having cybersex where neither of them considers it 'real,' despite arousal, a feeling of intimacy, and even mutual orgasm—and yet their real-life partners may beg to differ." Kolmes adds, "But it's fascinating that two people can be having an experience and one person may compartmentalize it in a way that feels 'not real,' while the other person is feeling much more integrated about it."

For Ellie Lumpesse, (lumpesse.com), it's sex all right—and thank goodness, because that's what she and her committed, live-in boyfriend of three years are openly looking for. She occasionally engages in cybersex with multiple partners on her own, and sometimes the couple has a cyber "threesome." The techno-poly couple is up front that the status of their relationship is nonmonogamous, but I still wondered how this nouveau poly arrangement negotiated the murky waters of cybersex and infidelity. Lumpesse explains, "Cheating is an interesting question. In my relationship we are incredibly open and honest. We don't have many rules, so there isn't much to lie about. Really, the only rule we have is to share what we are feeling and planning. So, for me, infidelity is taking an action or having a feeling that I think my partner would want to know but that I'm not telling him for some reason. I used to say that I 'don't do anything I wouldn't want him sitting next to me while I'm doing,' but I think that is pretty reductive and too prone to literal interpretation. Instead, any sort of keeping secrets feels like infidelity to me."

When Has a Line Been Crossed?

To Kolmes, this makes a lot of sense; cybersex outside a nonmonogamous relationship is a natural fit. "These kinds of different conceptions of the same sexual acts are not new for poly couples who may have very different feelings about various sensual, emotional, or sexual activities." . . . How this might work, Kolmes explains, "Some people may draw the line at cybersex with known people, saying that this would feel like too much of a violation, and that it's only okay if their partner plays with (presumed) strangers. Others may feel better having clear rules about sharing the logs of the activity. Some

"And whenever I attempt cybersex, my computer freezes."

"And whenever I attempt cybersex, my computer freezes," cartoon by Nick Downes, www.CartoonStock.com.

may want to watch or supervise. Some may prefer that the cybersex be around particular acts that are less appealing to them (fantasy play or sex acts that the partner may not enjoy as much). Others may feel more comfortable if their partner has cybersex using some other identity (gender-role switching, or via a virtual avatar, in a game, or whatever)."

But there's being OK with it, and there's not. We've all read the *Cosmo* articles about the fiancée who walked in on her almost-husband with his mouse in one hand and his—mouse—in the other, shockingly busting him having cybersex. (Yes, you read it. Continue.) To her this is a transgression, although it's likely not a clear one; it hurts, she feels jealous, betrayed, lied to, cheated on, and generally wonders if she's enough for him. But cybersex is layered and sometimes mysterious and complex. Unless he explains what's going on, it's tough to determine if it's healthy fantasy and masturbation (that is, if she's even OK with that concept), or having an actual sexual—or emotional—affair with another girl. He might have it tucked away in the "it's not about my *real* relationship" area of his psyche, but for her it is. The difficulty in cybersex and monogamy . . . is knowing when a line's been crossed.

How do you know if you're crossing a cybersex line? Talking about your cybersexuality with your partner is the right thing to do, but yeah, like that's easy when it's been an ongoing thing, or you have a fetish you don't know how (or want) to share. But if you're monogamous and having cybersex with someone who's not your partner, you need to know how to tell when the line's been crossed. Some advise that if it feels like cheating, it likely is. But Kolmes reminds us that it isn't that cut-and-dried, helpfully advising what to look for. "Signs that you may be crossing a line would include things like feeling guilty about it or feeling the need to keep it a secret. Or if you find that you're using cybersex as a safe way to express specific fantasies with someone that you are afraid to share with your relationship partner(s). Complaining about your relationship to the person you're engaging in cybersex with or using it in some way to devalue your relationship would also be signs that you are crossing boundaries. Canceling out on other face-to-face engagements with people in your life in order to have cybersex *could* be a bad sign."

Cybersex as Sex Toy

For better or for worse, there is no restart or reload for relationships; once you find yourself through the looking glass of cybersex and possible (or actual) violation of your relationship's ToS, it's time to talk. Kolmes suggests, "If you want to start talking about cybersex after you may have crossed some boundaries, it might be good to start by talking about fantasies and other erotic supplements to your fantasy life (such as pictures, videos, written erotica, toys)." Just talking about sex in general, Kolmes says, "would be a good launching point for acknowledging that there haven't been conversations about using more interactive media or involving other live people. If these types of conversations feel too intimidating, or they are not going well, it might be useful to consider getting help from a sex-positive therapist who works with people in relationships. It is also important to find a therapist who won't jump directly to assuming that this is a case of porn addiction or Internet addiction—but to find someone who can help you and your partner communicate more explicitly about fantasy, desires and about how to talk about these things."

However, not everyone is going to be wigged out by a little online canoodling. Some might think it's kinda hot, or even a new sex toy for the couple to share and add to the buffet of sexual activities the couple already enjoys. For these couples, Lumpesse speaks from experience when it comes to surfing the cybersex seas from within a relationship. "I probably have more than one piece of advice for couples," she adds. . . . "The . . . thing I would tell people to consider is that jealousy might not be the most important emotion they ever have. I still get jealous all the time, I've just learned that it is a fleeting response and I don't have to let it dictate my actions and decisions."

That said, we'll see how things go when I take the Virtual Boyfriend for a test drive. If I don't have any dishes left, I'll be re-shelving my copy of *A Brief History of Time* with the rest of the erotica.

Periodical and Internet Sources Bibliography

The following articles have been selected to supplement the diverse views presented in this chapter.

| Christina Caron | "Teen Sexting Linked to Psychological Distress," *ABC News*, November 10, 2011. |

Jacqui Cheng — "Predictors for Real Life Infidelity Include Cybersex, Sexting," *Ars Technica*, June 20, 2011. http://arstechnica.com.

Perry Chiaramonte — "In Fight Against Teen Sexting, Lawmakers Work to Avoid Turning Kids into Criminals," *FoxNews.com*, March 5, 2012.

Gregory Ferenstein — "Teenage Sexting Is Becoming the Norm," *TechCrunch*, July 6, 2012. http://techcrunch.com.

Emma Gray — "Adult Sexting: Does It Help or Hurt Relationships?," *Huffington Post*, April 20, 2012.

Lisa Mirza Grotts — "Online Dating Etiquette," *Huffington Post*, February 28, 2012.

Jessica Leshnoff — "Sexting Not Just for Kids," *AARP.org*, June 2011.

Judith Levine — "What's the Matter with Teen Sexting?," *American Prospect*, January 30, 2009.

Susan Lipkins — "Over 27? Be Wary," *Room for Debate* (blog), *New York Times*, June 9, 2011.

Christie Nicholson — "Why Online Dating Doesn't Work," *Scientific American*, February 18, 2012.

Brendan L. Smith — "Are Internet Affairs Different?," *Monitor on Psychology*, vol. 42, no. 3, March 2011.

OPPOSING
VIEWPOINTS®
SERIES

CHAPTER 4

What Are the Etiquette and Ethics of Social Media?

Chapter Preface

New technologies, such as television or video games or the Internet, often provoke public concern, as people worry about how or whether these media will affect society.

Social media have generated their share of worries. For example, in an April 14, 2009, *Daily Mail* article, Jenny Hope reports on a scientific study that suggested that Twitter and Facebook might make their users immoral. Scientists at the University of Southern California, Hope explains, had found that the quick news flashes and updates of social media sites move past too quickly for the brain to process morally. The scientists worried that social media users might become "indifferent to human suffering," because they do not have time to fully understand the moral aspects of the information they receive, or to empathize with those who are suffering. According to Antonio Damasio, the leader of the study, as quoted in Hope's article, "Lasting compassion in relationship to psychological suffering requires a level of persistent, emotional attention. In a media culture in which violence and suffering becomes an endless show, be it in fiction or in infotainment, indifference to the vision of human suffering gradually sets in."

In an April 14, 2009, post on the *Techdirt* blog, Mike Masnick argues that the actual results of the study were far less disturbing than Hope claims. According to Masnick, the study showed that "if you *only* interact with people through short bursts of information," it is harder to gauge the emotional affect of what is being said. In other words, people may respond less morally while on social media. However, that does not necessarily mean that social media are making formerly moral people less moral.

In fact, in an April 19, 2009, article on *Science Daily*, Damasio suggests that he is less concerned about social media in particular than about the way the culture in general presents suffering as entertainment in quick, jumping bursts. "What I'm more worried about," he said, "is what is happening in the (abrupt) juxtapositions that you find, for example, in the news." Social media for Damasio, then, seems to be part of broader social and media trends that may make it harder for people to act morally, but social media are not themselves a driving force behind a new wave of immorality.

The viewpoints in this chapter examine various issues related to the etiquette and ethics of social media, including perspectives on the morality and ethics of Facebook's relationship with its users.

> *"We are digital sharecroppers, but it's not our work lives being exploited for the gain of others, it's our personal lives."*

Facebook Immorally Exploits Its Users

Kevin Kelleher

Kevin Kelleher is a writer whose work has appeared in the New York Times, Fortune, Wired, *and other venues. In the following viewpoint, he argues that Facebook cynically invades its users' privacy and then sells the information it gains. He says that Facebook's disdain for its users is shown in the way it handled its first stock offering. He claims Facebook manipulated the offering so that users would never be majority owners of the company, and that it also provided potential purchasers of stock with misleading information. He concludes that Facebook treats its users with contempt while claiming to be improving their lives.*

As you read, consider the following questions:

1. What does Kelleher say were the pros and cons of Microsoft?

Kevin Kelleher, "Facebook, the Most Cynical Tech Giant Ever," Reuters.com, May 25, 2012. All rights reserved. Republication or redistribution of Thomson Reuters content, including by framing or similar means, is expressly prohibited without the prior written consent of Thomson Reuters. Thomson Reuters and its logo are registered trademarks or trademarks of the Thomson Reuters group of companies around the world. © Thomson Reuters 2012. Thomson Reuters journalists are subject to an Editorial Handbook which requires fair presentation and disclosure of relevant interests.

2. According to Kelleher, where did Facebook announce its lower revenue projections in the run-up to its IPO?

3. What did Mark Zuckerberg say that Facebook's mission was and was not, according to Kelleher?

For all its vaunted idealism, Silicon Valley can be just as cynical as any other area of commerce. The tech companies set up to profit from spam and search-engine trickery are too numerous to count. But Facebook's short history makes one thing clear: There has never been a tech company that built so much fortune from the exploitation of ordinary people while giving so little in return.

Using Users

Yes, Microsoft was vilified—and rightly so—for crushing competitors and forcing customers into an inferior operating-system software, but its iron-fisted dominance helped shape an immature and inchoate computer-software industry into a single standard that made PCs [personal computers] everyday devices in offices and homes. Microsoft's brutal strong-arm tactics were directed at rivals. Its sin against its customers was that its software, for decades, just wasn't that good.

Facebook, by contrast, built the best social network of its time, so good it left rivals like Myspace in the dust. And that should have been enough to make Facebook a Silicon Valley success story. Once it came time to make money, Facebook exploited its users' personal data to a degree that no company had ever achieved before.

Over the years, Facebook has curtailed some of its more blatantly exploitative practices, but only after a string of controversies forced its hand. It reluctantly let users control their privacy settings, and then it had to simplify those settings after many found them unnecessarily complex. (Some say they're still too complex.)

Facebook also backed off changes in its terms of service that allowed it to license users' data even after they left the site. But even now, regulators are objecting to Facebook's insistence that users grant the company a "non-exclusive, transferable, sub-licensable, royalty-free, worldwide license" to any photo, video or passing thought they see fit to publish on the site. Facebook has not only redefined the social web—it's redefining the very definition of "sharing."

Even if Facebook has lost some privacy battles, it still seems to be winning the war on private moments. It has, as one of its earliest backers wished, conditioned users to accept the creepiness of advertisers stalking their personal lives. And Facebook just keeps raising the creepiness bar.

But why must we users be used this way? It's not because we all long to be closet exhibitionists for Madison Avenue, but only because it pays a handsome profit to Facebook and its early investors. We are digital sharecroppers, but it's not our work lives being exploited for the gain of others, it's our personal lives. One out of every 5 cents of revenue Facebook brings in goes to its bottom line. We have handed the fruits of our labor over to Goldman Sachs, Digital Sky, Accel Partners[1] and [Mark] Zuckerberg [the head of Facebook] himself. And in return we get memories that Facebook expects to license and sub-license.

Users, Not Owners

It used to be that a successful Silicon Valley start-up would aspire to share its success with the customers who helped create it. Not long ago, investment gurus would counsel people to "invest in what you know"—and this would be sane advice. But in the era of Facebook, that advice is nonsense: Facebook is so cynical it doesn't even trust its own users to also be owners of the company (as some have sensibly suggested).

---

1. Goldman Sachs is a global investment bank; Digital Sky is an international investment firm; Accel Partners is a global venture and growth equity firm.

Trust and Mark Zuckerberg

As an undergraduate student at Harvard, [Mark] Zuckerberg worked for Divya Narendra and Cameron and Tyler Winklevoss on a social network called ConnectU. After his experiences at ConnectU, Zuckerberg created Facebook, but was sued by his former boss on the grounds that he stole ConnectU's source code to create Facebook. So, his first accusation of white-collar crime was for copyright infringement (or theft of computer codes). Eventually, the parties reached an out-of-court settlement where ConnectU was sold to Facebook and the owners were given $65 million, with much of the payment being in the form of shares in Facebook. . . .

It was eventually determined that all the settlement was paid in cheaper shares (known as preferred shares) rather than more expensive shares (known as common shares). The result—the original owners appealed the out-of-court settlement and accused Zuckerberg of securities fraud. So, his second accusation of white-collar crime arose. . . . Interestingly, while these allegations were being reviewed, some unwelcome information about Zuckerberg surfaced. While a 19-year-old Harvard student, Zuckerberg instant messaged a college friend the following comments about the information social networkers sent in to be posted on ConnectU: "People just submitted it. I don't know why. They 'trust' me. Dumb fu***s". The instant message he sent years ago came to light while Facebook users were criticizing the site for its lax privacy policies. Thus, a third possible allegation of white-collar crime has surfaced—misuse of computer information.

Brian K. Payne, "Section VII: Crime in the Economic and Technological Systems," White-Collar Crime: A Text/Reader. Thousand Oaks, CA: Sage, 2012, p. 241.

Zuckerberg did all he could to keep his users from being his company's owners. Three years ago, he sought—and won—a regulatory exemption that allowed his company to remain out of public ownership. Once it was inevitable that Facebook would have to go public [because of its large number of shareholders], Zuckerberg made sure the site's users could never have voting control over the company built on the content they created.

Confronted with the mundane reality of a publicly traded company, Facebook revealed the true depths of its cynicism. The company didn't trust its users to vote on its future. Zuckerberg disdained Wall Street as if he were an Occupy protester.[2] He wore a hoodie to road shows—a gesture that would carry more weight if he weren't in the upper echelons of the 1 percent, [that is, among the wealthiest 1 percent]. Facebook snickered at would-be investors by making them wait in line for a road show, then making them watch a 30-minute video that could have easily been posted on YouTube.

It was all a terrific joke, except for one thing: Facebook was every bit as arrogant—if not more arrogant—than the Wall Street firms it looked down on. Zuckerberg the hacker was taking the piss out of the financial elite—but somehow he had forgotten he was now part of the financial elite. Maybe that's why he seems to have handed the details of the IPO [initial public offering of stock] to his underlings, and that's where he went wrong.

There is much discussion of who's to blame for epic mishaps of the Facebook IPO, but this much seems evident: A week before the stock's debut, Facebook declared its revenue in the current quarter would be lower than it expected because more users were logging in through mobile devices, where it serves fewer ads. Facebook didn't announce this on its blog—where users who wanted to invest in the IPO could

2. Occupy Wall Street was a 2012 movement protesting inequality.

see it—but on page 57 of a 208-page document, the sixth revision of its IPO prospectus.

Given the importance of this pre-IPO disclosure, it felt weirdly opaque. It used insider jargon like "DAU" and "immaterial number of sponsored stories" before referring investors to an even more obscure section of the prospectus. Luckily for underwriters, Facebook actively notified them it was lowering its growth forecasts. Underwriters would in turn inform their favored clients.

Meanwhile, most Facebook users who wanted in on the IPO were stuck with parsing legalese inserted discreetly at the 11th hour. This is taking technicalities to the extreme: Expecting a typical Facebook user to figure out a financial reality that had to be explained to a Wall Street analyst is as cynical as it gets. And even worse: Despite its lowered revenue forecast, Facebook still increased the number of shares for sale (all of them sold by insiders, Facebook itself wouldn't get a cent) and raised the offering price.

Exploiting Its Visitors

Common sense says that if revenue is weakening before an IPO, the number of shares for sale as well as their price should fall. But not with Facebook, which looked on its users and investors with such derision it believed it could get away with anything. Mark Zuckerberg may have distanced himself from Facebook's IPO, but some strong leadership would have easily prevented this mess. Instead, as the saying goes, the fish stinks from the head: Leave your underlings to handle an IPO you dread, and they won't take it seriously either.

On the day of Facebook's IPO, Zuckerberg still claimed that Facebook's mission is not to be a public company, but to "make the world more open and connected." I get it: Facebook would love to remain private. But even so, Facebook isn't about its users. It's about exploiting its visitors. Listen to Zuckerberg's one-minute IPO speech, where he thanks "all the people out there who use Facebook and our products" and ends on a flat note. The tepid applause that follows is all you need to know about how Facebook thinks of you as a user or investor.

That speech reminded me of the infamous Zuckerberg IM [instant messaging] transcripts from the earliest days of Facebook, where he told a friend

i don't know why they "trust me" dumb fu---s.

In a 2010 profile, Zuckerberg said about that earlier exchange,

If you're going to go on to build a service that is influential and that a lot of people rely on, then you need to be mature, right? . . . I think I've grown and learned a lot.

Zuckerberg was right. He has indeed grown up. Not in the sense of outgrowing cynicism, but in the sense of learning how to harness a faith in the weakness of humanity into a multibillion-dollar company. And that's what's most cynical of all. It's one thing to profit from your customers—that's simple capitalism. It's another to exploit them so shamelessly, while claiming you're helping them to live better lives.

"Social media users are not only producers of social media but also consumers."

Facebook's Treatment of Its Users Is Not Especially Exploitive or Immoral

PJ Rey

PJ Rey is cofounder and co-organizer of the Cyborgology blog and the Theorizing the Web conference. In the following viewpoint, he argues that all capitalist companies exploit workers by taking some of the value they create for owners, or capitalists. According to Rey, this is true for factories as well as for Facebook. However, he says, Facebook is different than a factory in that users act as consumers as well as producers. Thus, it is difficult to tell how much Facebook users are exploited, since they are not only creating value but also consuming value. Rey concludes that Facebook users are exploited but not excessively or immorally compared to other companies.

As you read, consider the following questions:

1. According to Rey, how does Karl Marx describe exploitation?

PJ Rey, "Facebook Is Not a Factory (but Still Exploits Its Workers)," *Organizations, Occupations and Work*, February 22, 2012. Copyright © 2012 by PJ Rey. All rights reserved. Reproduced by permission.

2. According to Rey, how much money has Facebook netted from each user, and how does Rey suggest that figure could be used to estimate the degree to which Facebook is exploiting its users?

3. Why does Rey say that users should be skeptical of Mark Zuckerberg's claim that Facebook is not trying to make money?

Facebook's IPO [initial public offering] announcement [that it will become a publicly owned company] has stirred much debate over the question of whether Facebook is exploiting/using/taking advantage of its users. The main problem with the recent discussion of this subject is that no one really seems to have taken the time to actually define what exploitation is. Let me start by reviewing this concept before proceeding to examine its relevance to Facebook.

Defining Exploitation

The concept of exploitation came to prominence about a century and a half ago through the writings of Karl Marx, and he gave it a specific, objectively calculable definition—though, I'll spare you the mathematical expressions. Marx starts from the assumption that value is created from labor (most people today acknowledge that value is contingent on other factors as well, but we need merely to accept that labor is one source of value for Marx's argument to work). According to Marx, humans have an important natural relationship to the fruits of our labor, and our work is a definitive part of who we are. Modern capitalist society is unique from other periods in history because workers sell their labor time in exchange for wages (as opposed to, say, creating objects and bartering them for other objects). Capitalists accumulate money by skimming off some of the value created by a worker's labor, so the wages a worker receives are only a fraction of the total value he or she has created. The portion of the value created by a worker that is not returned back to that worker (after operating costs are covered) is called the *rate of exploitation.*

So, for example, imagine that, during one day of work, a factory worker takes $10 worth of wood and assembles a chair that retails for $60; if the worker is paid $20 in wages for that day, then rate of exploitation would equal $30/day. That is to say, the capitalist is made $30 richer each day at the expense of the worker. The *real degree of exploitation,* however, is best represented in relative terms. If we calculate the $30 of surplus value expropriated by the capitalist as a percentage of the total value created ($60 − $10 = $50), then we find that the real degree of exploitation is 60% of the value created by the worker.

The important point here is that exploitation is an objective calculation—one that is separable from the subsequent moral debates we often have about ensuring fairness versus rewarding risk/innovation. So, if we want to have a debate about the (im)morality of Facebook's business model—as many recent commentators are, in fact, endeavoring to do—we must first establish that exploitation objectively exists on Facebook. However, this is not as easy as it might seem. The organization of Facebook hardly resembles the "cattle-like existence" in the factories that Marx originally set out to describe. While Facebook's users flock to the site willingly, even happily, Marx summarized the factory as a place where the worker:

> does not feel content but unhappy, does not develop freely his physical and mental energy but mortifies his body and ruins his mind. . . . His labor is therefore not voluntary, but coerced; it is forced labor. It is therefore not the satisfaction of a need; it is merely a means to satisfy needs external to it. Its alien character emerges clearly in the fact that as soon as no physical or other compulsion exists, labor is shunned like the plague.

Given this apparent disconnect between the experience of factory work and social media use, we should be reluctant about merely attempting to superficially shoehorn this new phenomenon into the classic conceptual frame of exploitation. Instead, we should ask ourselves if these apparent differences have any bearing on the assumptions underlying our calculation of the rate of exploitation. Indeed, a closer examination reveals significant differences between the way exploitation is carried out in the factory and on social media.

Why Do People Use Social Media Voluntarily, but Avoid Factory Work?

There are two important reasons: 1.) Factory work is alienating, separating workers from their creative faculties to shape the nature of the objects they are laboring to produce. Social media encourage a much greater degree of self-directed creativity. 2.) Social media users are not only producers of social media but also consumers. As such, there are direct and obvious benefits to social media use, unlike the discomfort of factory work which [is] only partially and indirectly remediated by wages. These benefits of social media use are largely immaterial: e.g., making and preserving social connections, cultivating and demonstrating taste, and telegraphing that you are "with it," part of the in crowd. (Sociologists call these benefits cultural, social, and symbolic capital.)

Though we all can recognize that these immaterial benefits have real value, it is extremely difficult to fix a price to them. How many dollars is a friendship worth? How much cultural literacy can you purchase for $100? Moreover, because usage patterns vary so widely, different social media users are bound to derive different sorts of value from their use. That is to say, the value of these immaterial benefits is relative to the unique circumstances of each user. Because users are "compensated" through these immaterial benefits (rather than receiving conventional wages), it is extremely difficult to come up with a

165

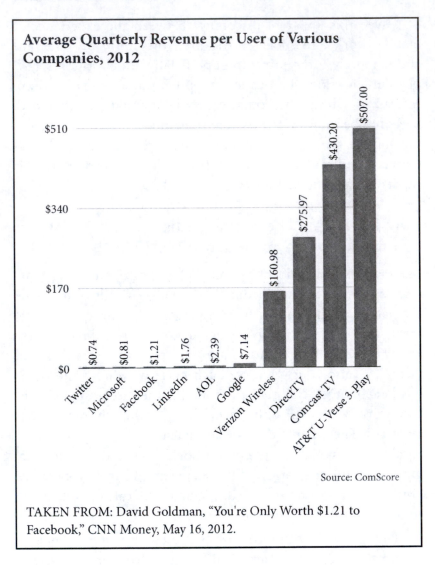

Average Quarterly Revenue per User of Various Companies, 2012

Twitter: $0.74
Microsoft: $0.81
Facebook: $1.21
LinkedIn: $1.76
AOL: $2.39
Google: $7.14
Verizon Wireless: $160.98
DirectTV: $275.97
Comcast TV: $430.20
AT&T U-Verse 3-Play: $507.00

Source: ComScore

TAKEN FROM: David Goldman, "You're Only Worth $1.21 to Facebook," CNN Money, May 16, 2012.

concrete figure for the real degree of exploitation. (Note: This is not really "compensation" because this value is created directly by and shared between users.) We know that Facebook receives all the material benefits from our use. Most readers have probably already seen it calculated that with 850 million users and a speculative valuation of $100 billion, Facebook has netted $117.65 from each user. In this sense, we might say that the rate of exploitation is $117.65 per user for the eight years that Facebook has been in existence. However, without a concrete figure for the total value produced by each user, we are not really able to derive the real degree of exploitation. The best we can do is a sort of thought experiment: Would I pay $117.65 for what I have gotten out of Facebook in the past several years? If the answer is yes (personally speaking, I know I pay that much *annually* to host a website that I use far less than my profile), then we can loosely infer that the real degree of exploitation is less than 50%.

Why Does It Matter That Exploitation Is Less than 50%?

Many critics of social media downplay the immaterial benefits of social media and argue that, because workers do not receive wages, they are experiencing "over-exploitation" (i.e., a condition where the real degree of exploitation approaches 100%). Our little thought experiment enables us to conclude that, while Facebook is exploitative (like all capitalist enterprise), it does not appear to be substantially more exploitative than conventional "brick-and-mortar" businesses. While all the alarm about hyper-capitalism and the precarious state of social media users is probably overstated, the fundamentally exploitative nature of Facebook's business model gives users ample cause to be skeptical of the benevolent image of Facebook that founder and CEO [chief executive officer] Mark Zuckerberg painted in the IPO letter, saying "We don't build services to make money; we make money to build better services." Unfortunately for users, the fuzziness surrounding these economic relationships may make it easier than ever inducing this sort of "false consciousness."

> "After many years of an unbroken record of not biting on spam, viruses or phishing attempts, I was taken."

Social Media Users Should Practice Good Netiquette in Dealing with Spam

Suzanne Choney

Suzanne Choney is a writer, editor, and producer at MSNBC .com. In the following viewpoint, she discusses her embarrassment at having clicked on, and therefore forwarded, a spam Twitter message to her followers. She says that people need to be careful not to forward spam or click on suspicious links. If they do click on such links, she says, they should notify others quickly to help them avoid the scam. Choney concludes by urging people to always include explanations with their links so real links are identifiable and spam links may be more easily recognized.

As you read, consider the following questions:

1. What was the spam scam that caught Choney, and why does she say she was susceptible to it?

Suzanne Choney, "How to Apologize After Spreading Spam," MSNBC.com, February 23, 2010. Copyright © 2010. Reproduced with permission of MSNBC Interactive News LLC. via Copyright Clearance Center.

2. What does Landesman say are the ABCs of proper etiquette to follow when there's a social networking scam?

3. According to Choney, what are phishing attempts?

Love may mean never having to say you're sorry, but not so with certain vicious kinds of spam that can lead to compromised online accounts, especially on social networking sites like Twitter and Facebook, where more and more of us are congregating these days.

"LOL—Is This You?"

After many years of an unbroken record of not biting on spam, viruses or phishing [referring to a scam to acquire information about a user by masquerading as a trustworthy entity or business] attempts, I was taken. I'm not proud to admit it, but there it is. Over the weekend, a direct message, or "DM" on Twitter from a work colleague caught my attention: "LOL—is this you?" with a link to click on.

What was he referring to? Something I'd written? A photo that shouldn't be online, but was? I couldn't imagine what it might be, but an irrational fear of something humiliating— and the fact it was sent on a weekend—propelled me to click on the link. And now, I truly am humiliated, apologizing to several people who are connected to me on Twitter who got the same bogus message, but from me—just like I got it from the work colleague who inadvertently clicked on the link.

Many of us live more and more of our lives online these days, from time to time "Googling" our own names to check any chatter, good or bad. We're told we can't be too careful about what we say or the photos we post. Perhaps that's why the "is this you?" question struck a nerve.

I've written about "phishing" expeditions many a time, and now I'd gone and helped propagate one. I've also received my fair share of "don't click on this link—my account was hijacked/hacked" e-mails from others via Facebook. Among the most recent was a Valentine's Day phishing attempt.

"Please do not open any valentine messages from me, although I do wish everyone a happy valentines day," was the message from the real Facebook friend who sent a warning.

"Too Quick to Click"

"People are too quick to click" on links, Mary Landesman, senior security researcher for ScanSafe, had told me last spring. And she was right. But how to right the wrong?

> *"Ack—just learned this: DMs (direct messages) to you w/link to Twitter is possible virus; DO NOT click on link and log in! Lks like accts r being hijacked,"* I tweeted Saturday, using the 140-character limit of Twitter, then sending this as a follow-up message:

> *". . . If not virus, may be phishing effort to get your log-in, and lede-in will say: 'LOL . . . is this you?' or some such . . ."*

Still, not everybody checks their Twitter account all the time, and messages do pile up. Mine got buried by Sunday, when I received some messages marked by irritation and concern asking whether I was aware I had sent this potentially dangerous link.

Another round of tweets from me went out Sunday: *"Tweeted this yest, but will say again today, as I was 'bitten'—Do NOT click on links in DMs from me or anyone that start 'LOListhisyou?'"* with a follow-up message from Twitter's own @safety account, saying, "If you think your account has been phished, check out our help page for compromised accounts."

I contacted Landesman of ScanSafe, which provides web security as a service to businesses, telling her my experience. She says there are "ABCs of proper etiquette" to follow when there's a social networking scam:

> Acknowledge the attack to anyone who might have been adversely impacted.

Be detailed—tell them what message they might have received as a result of the malware/phishing and what might have happened as a result.

Caution your contacts—use this as an opportunity to remind everyone that just because you think a message came from someone you know, there really is no way of telling for sure. If they ever do click a link that then leads to a log-in page or to a video codec install, they should close the page immediately and contact their friend via some other method to inquire (and possibly alert them) about the seemingly malicious link.

She acknowledges that Twitter, "with its 140 characters limitation, makes it a bit harder. For that medium, and specific to (last) weekend's Twitter attack, your best bet would be a tweet saying something along the lines of:

'If you revd "Lol—this is me/funny/you," don't click. It's a phishing scam. If you fell for it too, change your pw. I'm very sorry.:("'

"For more generic Twitter malware and phishing apologies, the gist of it should include enough details about the message sent so folks can identify it, ended with a brief 'I'm sorry,'" she said.

Don't Include the Link

One thing an apology should not include: the troublesome link itself.

"Don't ever include a link in the apology," she says. "After all, it was clicking on a link that got folks in trouble in the first place."

Phishing attempts—which seek to get your log-in information as a way of trying to snoop around and get bank account numbers or any other personal information that can be used in identity theft—have been plentiful on Facebook as well as Twitter.

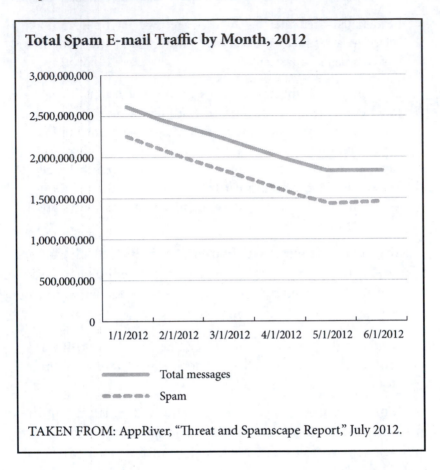

Total Spam E-mail Traffic by Month, 2012

Total messages

Spam

TAKEN FROM: AppRiver, "Threat and Spamscape Report," July 2012.

The "LOL—is that you?" attempt not only struck Twitter users last weekend, but those of social networking site Bebo .com, according to security firm Sophos.

The company noted on its blog that in its recent "Security Threat Report" covering the last year, there has been "an astonishing 70 percent rise in the number of users reporting spam and malware attacks via social networks."

The use of shortened web links—for example, http://bit.ly/ 9HBegt—are especially helpful when using sites like Twitter, but are also more fraught with peril because they disguise what could be a bogus site. In this case, that link goes to a real story on MSNBC.com.

"It would greatly help if people got out of the habit of sending very short messages with links," Landesman advises.

"Instead, get in the habit of including some identifying info so that the recipient can tell that you really did intend to send it. For example, instead of sending 'Check out this funny video,' always include more specifics like, 'Funny video—reminds me of that crazy guy we saw on the beach in the Bahamas.'

"If enough folks adopted this habit, it would become much easier to distinguish the really generic messages as being likely phishing or malware attacks."

| *"Are online ethics so flimsy that a single company's culture can alter them?"*

Using Bots and Automation Can Be Akin to Spamming

Adam Justice

Adam Justice is a web developer and online journalist whose work has appeared on Yahoo! News. In the following viewpoint, he says that on social media platforms, automation and bots— software applications that run automated tasks—were traditionally considered unethical. Such applications were thought to give some users an unfair advantage and were frowned upon. However, Justice says, Twitter has allowed and even encouraged the use of bots and automation. Justice says that Twitter has damaged online etiquette and has made it harder to prosecute and stop spammers.

As you read, consider the following questions:

1. What does Justice say was the most important factor in demonstrating that bot use was unethical before Twitter?

2. What advantages do supplementary Twitter applications give you over the official interface, according to Justice?

Adam Justice, "Twitter Ethics: Lawsuits, Spam-Bots, and You," *Social Media Sun*, http://socialmediasun.com. Copyright © by Adam Justice. All rights reserved. Reproduced by permission.

3. What statistics does Justice cite to show that there is too much automation on Twitter?

Twitter announced last week that they planned to tighten restrictions on spamming and automation. Normally this is publicly considered good news by everyone affected, but there have been several bloggers and pundits denounce the move. Instead of increasing penalties or targeting the actual spammers, Twitter has filed lawsuits against five third-party developers who were involved in the creation of automated spamming tools. The most well-known of which is Tweet Adder.

Automation Makes a Re-Tweet Spam

It all comes down to ethics. At the heart of the bloggers' argument is that a small group of spammers are misusing the tools that help "marketers" plan and execute their social media campaigns. This is a completely backward view that social networkers and every kind of online community has had since public Internet access became available: that when developers launched an application, ethical use only included use that originated from the application's own proprietary interface.

Using a program that gave you an undue advantage was even worse. Before there was Tweet Adder, there was adding trains, Friend Blaster, macros and a whole other assortment of automation tools to use on everything from Myspace to Yahoo! chat rooms. They were universally known to be unethical, and many of the advantages are the same you'll get from a program like HootSuite and TweetDeck.

The fact is that the ethics involved with automation and bot use [referring to the use of software applications that run automated tasks] have been skewed for the past couple years. Social media platforms can place blame on whomever they want, but there is one culprit who deserves much more blame—a social network named Twitter.

As recently as three years ago, practically all Internet users agreed on the ethical problems with bot use. Those that didn't understand the ethical implications entirely still knew that there was something inherently wrong with using a different interface to access applications and games that gave the user a decided advantage over their counterparts. Most importantly, the people who did use bots didn't admit it. Rather than face public criticism, they kept it to themselves and forced the platforms to bust them, and then take the necessary disciplinary actions. Denial confirmed the notion that it was unethical and that the user knew it.

It was around this time that Twitter started to get bigger. With the integration of mobile and the unique aspects of the 140-character micro blog, Twitter allowed third-party developers to openly distribute applications that had the ability to totally replace the Twitter interface.

Up until that point, the only accepted programs were aggregators that could combine several platforms into a single interface. Some Twitter users had several thousand followers, and were following several thousand accounts themselves. It made sense to allow programs to optimize the experience any way they could. The bots became "tools" to users, scheduling [that is, scheduling tweets or posts for delayed appearance] became a popular practice, and automation started to become accepted. At least at first, users remembered that there was something inherently wrong with having an advantage over other users.

When Does a Tool Become Black Hat?

Social media, and especially Facebook and Twitter, were becoming more popular by the day. The regular black hats had their bots and macros, but as the lines blurred between the capabilities of a tool like TweetDeck and a bot like Tweet Adder, regular users began taking advantage of programs that were explicitly allowed, although limited, in Twitter's end-user license agreement. After all, why wouldn't they? It is playing by Twitter's own rules, and there you can do a lot of cool things with the right program.

Social media marketing experts who were looking for an edge stumbled upon the more powerful tools, and it wasn't long before they were recommending them in their books and even selling them as an affiliate on their websites. Twitter condoned it all for the most part; they just asked that users keep automation to a reasonable amount.

As users who weren't familiar with the wars that prior social networks and other platforms had fought against bots and macros in the past started taking to Twitter en mass. The lure of social proof and potential profits from garnering a massive following was more than enough [to] lead them on a search for the tools that could replicate the success that others were having.

Since Tweet Adder allowed users to make a sizeable commission from each sale, the active networkers weren't even trying to keep it a secret. What's more striking is the fact that it was no longer taboo; people were recommending it publicly and hardly anyone denounced it. Twitter was still growing at a spectacular pace, so why police something that helps inflate your user numbers so much?

The current crop of bots and Twitter apps are popular because they can automate actions on social networks that lead to growth. The growth can be transformed into added engagement, and the engagement can lead to profit. Is all fair in love and money? Greed has allowed the use of automated Twitter accounts to blossom among users just the same as it allowed Twitter itself to turn a blind eye to their users who were both padding the numbers and flooding the network simultaneously.

You can't argue that the whole idea of supplementary Twitter applications is to give you distinct advantages over the official interface. You can reach followers on the other side of the planet who would normally be asleep during your active hours, you can multiply the number of actions you're capable of completing on any given day, you can live a normal life and still portray yourself as a Twitter super user, and you can use advanced filters to make it all more efficient. The question isn't whether or not it works, it's whether having access to the social networking equivalent of steroids is ethical; and since it isn't ethical, how could all of the professionals, and Twitter themselves, turn a blind eye for so long?

Ethics and Convenience

Growth has slowed for Twitter, and it's obvious that they have a spam and bot problem. When five percent of users are responsible for 75 percent of all tweets, you know there is a little too much automation going on. So now that they've plateaued, they need to curb the use of such programs before they can reach a larger audience. Even though marketers who frequent the same "Warrior Forum" that hackers and bot enthusiasts frequented five years ago have accepted wide scale use of automation, the general public still gets an icky feeling when they find out that they are the only ones present at a party that is seemingly jumping. People don't like to be fed by robots, and Twitter knows it.

Applications like Twitter are best if ALL users are limited to the same user interface that was developed as part of the application. The user experience is better; it puts users on equal footing and removes automated spam altogether. Twitter's acceptance of all these programs that can post to their platform is an Internet first. They relinquished that control, and that's why I don't see them winning a lawsuit for that very reason. They didn't create this monster, but they invited [it] to stay in their home and fed it high protein gruel. Now that it's as big as it has ever been, it's going to be nearly impossible to eradicate. When a user sees other people exploiting "tools" at every available opportunity, they aren't going to stand idle while others are passing them by.

Even if Twitter wins all five lawsuits, users are so used to using automation and bots that they'll search fervently for a replacement and a programmer will reach out to meet that demand in spite of prior lawsuits. Some users will try and compromise and justify it; even though your average marketing disciple is plenty smart, the prevailing culture has warped their sense of ethics.

I'll be honest here: Even though I recognize the ethical conundrum we face when using a superior interface, I've always felt like ethics are better saved for serious matters. I don't care if you sent your tweet from Buffer, TweetDeck, the official Twitter app or from your iPad in the bathroom. I accept the current culture of tweet-botting and scheduling, and as long as average users don't form a mob, I won't try and hide my use of programs like Buffer, Triberr and IFTTT.

Do you use automation in your social media strategy? Have you ever had a strategy that didn't involve some level of automation or scheduling? No matter what anyone says, it is historically unethical. The question is why do we let convenience dictate when the platforms write the rules? Are online ethics so flimsy that a single company's culture can alter them? And how important is it to maintain ethics when the crime is spam—nonviolent, and some would say victimless. If you were the judge, do you rule in favor of Twitter, who has obviously had a change of heart due to their bottom line—or do you rule in favor of the third-party apps that spent time developing programs that were accepted by everyone at the time, even though they wouldn't have been a few years prior?

"*Nobody should make the mistake in believing that social media background checks are merely a passing fad—they are the wave of the future.*"

Employees Should Accept the Growing Use of Social Media Background Checks

Michael Rainey

Michael Rainey is the editor of INSIGHT Into Diversity *magazine. In the following viewpoint, he says that companies are increasingly performing social media background checks as a way to evaluate prospective employees. Rainey says that inappropriate pictures or even status updates can damage an applicant's chance at a job. He argues that employers are going to continue using social media background checks, and employees need to be aware of the danger. He also argues that social media can be used to help, rather than hinder, a job search. He concludes that users of social media should not post anything that would discourage a potential employer from hiring them.*

As you read, consider the following questions:

1. What percentage of employers use social media background checks, according to Rainey?

Michael Rainey, "Social Media Background Checks," *INSIGHT Into Diversity*, February 15, 2012. http://www.insightintodiversity.com. Copyright © 2012 by Michael Rainey. All rights reserved. Reproduced by permission.

2. What example does Rainey give of uses of social media background checks that is illegal?

3. What does Rainey suggest is the best advice regarding questionable comments or photographs on social media?

That picture of you in a hot tub with a beer in your hand and two attractive females sitting next to you sure looks great as the profile picture on your Facebook page, but can it prevent you from getting a job? The answer, somewhat surprisingly, is yes. Employers have been doing standard background checks and credit reports on employees for decades, but in recent years hiring managers have also begun checking out the personal social media pages of candidates under consideration for a position, a practice known as "social media background checks," to determine as much as possible about a candidate before they hire them. The more pictures you have of yourself in compromising positions on Facebook and Twitter, the more damage you are doing to your employability status. Various reports suggest that between 50 and 90 percent of employers use social media background checks to vet out prospective employees.

Inappropriate Photographs and More

If you become a finalist or a semifinalist for an open position and a hiring manager comes across pictures of you carousing with your friends and appearing to be in various states of inebriation, they are going to be significantly less likely to hire you. The question becomes, is this newest form of candidate screening ethical?

"On the one hand, an employer could be putting themselves at risk because a person's behavior outside of work is their own business," says Vicky Ayers, the institutional services coordinator for RPA Inc. "On the other hand, if your boss were to walk into a restaurant and see you carousing and behaving in an embarrassing way and there was potential for a backlash against his business, would he have a right to be concerned about your behavior? I think he would. It's all up in the air right now. What constitutes private and personal today is very different than it was 10 years ago."

Social media background checks run much deeper than just employers seeking out inappropriate photographs. They are also reading status updates, checking employment-based social media websites like LinkedIn to see if a candidate's educational and employment background matches up with what their resume says, determining if there are any negative comments posted about a previous employer, etc. "If a candidate has applied for a position that has a communication component to it, an employer will check to see if the prospective employee presents themselves well from a communication standpoint—do they write well, do they communicate well?" says Jonathan T. Hyman, a Cleveland-based employment lawyer who is one of the authors of *Think Before You Click: Strategies for Managing Social Media in the Workplace*. "They may also check to see whether a candidate appears to be a good fit for corporate culture based on the image they portray online or whether they appear to be creative and have the right skill set. There's a whole bunch of information, both good and bad, that companies can mine these social media sites for."

Privacy Settings Are Not Enough

Facebook is notorious for having privacy settings where users can make their profiles only visible to "friends," but it would be wrong for somebody to assume that they can post whatever they want and prying eyes will never see it just because the privacy settings are turned on. "If you are considering John Doe for employment and you know that he is Facebook friends with an employee that you have, there's nothing to stop you from going to that employee and asking them to print off a copy of John Doe's profile for you to review," Hyman says. "There are ways around [privacy settings]. While

Facebook's privacy settings give the individual some sense of security, it can in a lot of cases be a false sense of security."

There have been instances where a company will ask a prospective employee if they can view their Facebook page before they hire them. While this gives the candidate in question a chance to "scrub" their profile of any incriminating content before the employer sees it, the chances of something falling through the cracks are too great. In short, if you are in the job market, you shouldn't post anything that could possibly prevent a company from hiring you. However, you aren't exactly home free even if you already have a job and aren't actively seeking a different one. Employees have been fired from their current jobs as a result of comments made on social media sites. . . .

Legally, existing antidiscrimination laws cover using social media to make hiring decisions based on race. For example, it would be illegal for an employer, in a search for Caucasian employees, to screen applicants by looking at their photos on Facebook, Twitter or LinkedIn to determine if they fit that predetermined criteria before interviewing them. The only actual law that covers background checks is the Fair Credit Reporting Act (FCRA), but it only sets up a series of procedural hoops that a company/employer has to jump through when it hires a consumer-reporting agency or third-party organization to conduct background checks for them. If the company/employer performs the background checks in-house, the FCRA never comes into play. "Everybody needs to walk on eggshells with this stuff because there aren't good laws to protect people," Ayers says.

Not a Fad

Nobody should make the mistake in believing that social media background checks are merely a passing fad—they are the wave of the future and figure to become even more prominent in the years to come. "It is definitely the future," Hyman says.

New Ethical Problems with Social Media

Social networking sites and other social media present new and thorny problems. What happens when an employee posts confidential company information on a public site? Is it okay to post sexual comments about a co-worker or your boss on a public site? This kind of behavior can reflect poorly on an employer as well as make the author of such comments look like an idiot or worse. The scariest part of this scenario is that items posted on the Internet last forever. You can't just "erase" them and ensure that they're really obliterated forever. Organizations take this behavior very seriously. One recent college graduate hired into a plum job by a national retailer was fired for posting inappropriate content about his employer on his Facebook wall.

Linda K. Trevino and Katherine A. Nelson,
"Addressing Individual's Common Ethical Problems,"
Managing Business Ethics: Straight Talk About How
to Do It Right, *5th ed. New York: John Wiley, 2011, p. 133.*

"In fact, with as many as 90 percent of companies doing this already, the future is very much here now."

If used properly, social media can help job seekers find the position they desire by allowing them to network and establish relationships with other professionals in their chosen field that they wouldn't ordinarily get a chance to meet. But like many new technological developments, social media can be an incredibly powerful tool in both a positive and negative sense. "For job seekers and employees, social media is very much a tool in reputational management," Hyman says. "Nobody would ever walk into a job interview with a Fortune 500 company wearing ripped jeans and flip-flops while holding a beer in their hand, but those are the pictures people have posted on their Facebook pages without their privacy settings locked down and anybody can type their name into the search bar on Facebook and look at those photos. Employees need to understand that employers are looking at this information and are making employment decisions based on this information.

"People need to take ownership of their image and how they portray themselves online. They need to embrace social media not just for the added connectivity, communication and ability to readily share, but also as an opportunity to control the message they are sending out about themselves to their current employers and to prospective employers."

It's possible for you to use your social media pages to communicate with friends and relatives while maintaining a clean, respectable image. The best advice a person can get regarding questionable photographs and comments they may be considering making public is "when in doubt, don't post it." It's always better to be safe than sorry.

"As my grandmother once told me: 'Fools' names and fools' faces are always seen in public places,'" Ayers advises. "Everyone should be very careful about what they put out in public."

> "I see the practice of social media vetting as akin to hiring a private detective to snoop on a candidate."

Employers Should Be Cautious About Using Social Media Background Checks

Personnel Today

Personnel Today *is an online magazine focusing on news and content for human resources professionals. The following viewpoint argues that using social media sites to screen candidates for employment is unnecessary and may be dangerous for employers. The viewpoint says that screening candidates based on personal information may leave employers open to legal action. The viewpoint concludes that employers need to be very cautious until the legal issues around the use of social media information obtained by employers have become clearer.*

As you read, consider the following questions:

1. How did the University of Kentucky get in legal trouble using social media vetting, according to the viewpoint?

"Social Media Background Checks a Minefield for Recruiters," PersonnelToday.com, September 15, 2011. Copyright © 2011 by Reed Business Information. All rights reserved. Reproduced by permission.

2. What warnings does Acas give about social network background checks?

3. Why does Jacqueline Wiltshire say that many online indiscretions are often best ignored?

At a time when social media profiles are the norm and many people are falling into the trap of "over-sharing" personal information online, it is perhaps inevitable that recruiters would be tempted to have a sneaky peek at the digital lives being led by potential recruits to their organisations.

In many cases, it is an easy opportunity to get an insight into the true character of the person who just aced their interview but who you still don't know much about.

Legal Quagmire

But the practice of using online research in hiring decisions could land employers in a legal quagmire and should be firmly resisted, according to a number of recruiters and lawyers.

One of them—Alex Rickard, head of employee proposition at law firm Towry—says that the only fair way to build web checks into the recruitment process is to "warn candidates of your intention and give them the chance to clean up their online profile before you get started".

As many as 70% of US recruiters have allegedly rejected candidates following social media checks carried out either by in-house recruitment staff or by third-party service providers. Of particular concern are online profiles linking candidates to extreme political views or to images of sexually explicit or illegal activity.

The prospect of British employers adding Facebook or YouTube research to either the general recruitment screening process or to the background checks that routinely follow job offers "should raise alarm bells both legally and ethically," says Sarah Gordon, associate director of the Sammons Group.

"I see the practice of social media vetting as akin to hiring a private detective to snoop on a candidate or perhaps paying someone to break into their home and rifle through their drawers. It isn't fair, it shouldn't be necessary and in my view, it's a trend that reputable employers should steer well clear of," Gordon says.

Turning down an apparently exemplary candidate following a social media check has already landed one US employer—the University of Kentucky—in trouble.

The university was forced to make a $125,000 out-of-court settlement to a UK-born scientist who, despite being the best fit for a director-level job, was turned down after being found to have expressed creationist views online—which were felt to conflict with the role he had applied for. This should be a warning to all employers not to experiment with web searching, says Sarah Beeby, senior associate at law firm SNR Denton.

"If a firm offer has been made, accepted and subsequently withdrawn after online vetting, there is certainly the potential for a candidate to claim damages and compensation, even if they cannot actually claim unfair dismissal."

Recommendations

This view echoes recommendations made by Acas [Advisory, Conciliation and Arbitration Service] recently, as it launched its first social media guide for employers. As well as offering guidelines on managing employees' use of social media, Acas suggested that companies checking on candidates via social networks leave themselves open to charges of discrimination, as they are likely to glean information ranging from sexual orientation and ethnicity to religion, age and political views, making it easier for rejected candidates to claim that they have been discriminated against.

While it may be unwise to make judgments about employability on the basis of someone's online comments or status updates, it is the issue of unsavory images that holds even more danger for employers, believes Beeby.

"By relying on potentially inaccurate web images that may have been 'tagged' to your candidate, you run a serious risk of discriminating against people; particularly if you turn someone down for a job after seeing images of them in a wheelchair, with their children, or perhaps attending a religious festival.

"It may be very tempting for employers to use Facebook and other sites to add another layer of screening to their recruitment process but if their existing procedures are robust enough, they really shouldn't need to run the enormous risks of probing too deeply into what are, in effect, purely social sites, whether directly or via a specialist search firm," she adds.

The fashion for uninhibited behaviour on the web is undoubtedly a gift for recruitment staff keen to know a little more about the views, motivations and lifestyles of job seekers, but according to Jacqueline Wiltshire, director of HR [human resources] and organisational development at Ealing Council, it's what an employer does with any resulting information that counts.

"There's nothing sneaky about recruitment managers having a quick look at people's profiles online, but we believe that formally using social networking sites at the screening stage is neither cost-effective nor useful and to use a third party to do it could lead to all sorts of inaccuracies over things like duplicate names."

The council already carries out a range of checks, either basic or enhanced, on issues such as claimed qualifications or benefits entitlement and if these unearth something the council isn't happy with, they go back to the individual and give them a chance to explain.

"I can only see online material being really relevant if it appears to utterly fly in the face of our codes of conduct—perhaps photographs of inappropriate behaviour with children by someone being hired to work in children's services, or evidence that an agency worker is not legally entitled to work for us," says Wiltshire.

"If something like that was brought to our attention, we would of course be forced to act and could of course withdraw any existing job offer."

Online Indiscretions Best Ignored

While the US experience thus far is that photos and videos tend to attract more alarm among recruiters than ill-conceived blogging or postings, Wiltshire believes that many online indiscretions are best ignored.

"To an extent, it depends on how senior the hire is; a CEO [chief executive officer] job perhaps demands greater care and attention than a junior admin position. But I think it's worth pointing out that even if we in HR don't like something we see about a candidate on a social networking site, we have to be grown up and accept that we need to fill positions and work with people who may have very different interests and private lives to our own.

"If we do become too puritanical about what people do in their private lives, we may find it difficult to fill certain jobs altogether," she adds.

Rickard agrees. "When it comes to most positions, we already have detailed CVs [curricula vitae] and subsequent checking procedures to find out as much as we need to know about a person before they begin working for us.

"If their online activity isn't strictly relevant to their ability to perform well, then I would guard against delving too deeply unless the post is a highly sensitive one."

Last year, the German parliament signalled its intention to draw a legal distinction between social networking sites such as Facebook and professional networks such as LinkedIn; effectively banning candidate vetting via the former but permitting employers to search using the latter.

While the resultant law has yet to be passed, Sarah Gordon believes that the UK may eventually be forced to follow Germany's lead.

"We all know that our LinkedIn profiles and postings may well be looked at as part of the recruitment process and, because it is so transparent, this strikes me as totally fair. But Facebook is a very different matter.

"While I hope that UK employers will fall short of using social networking to find out more about job seekers, I would urge all candidates to both understand and use the privacy settings on sites such as Facebook to screen out any potential snooping."

While social sites may pose the biggest danger to the naive and the unguarded, Gordon adds a warning to web users in general.

"We should all know by now we need to avoid those awful 'sexykitten@hotmail' e-mail addresses if we want to be taken more seriously by employers."

"But don't think that expressing strong views on X or Y via the LinkedIn discussion boards somehow doesn't count. These can be just as damaging to your professional reputation."

A final word goes to Sarah Beeby. "Our clients tell us that they're only just starting to understand how powerful social networking sites can be and they need to be guided.

"At this present time, the best advice is to adopt a watch-and-wait attitude until the various complex privacy issues around all these sites are fully resolved."

Periodical and Internet Sources Bibliography

The following articles have been selected to supplement the diverse views presented in this chapter.

Rob Enderle	"Unfriending Facebook: Anticipating the Revenge of the Facebook Ex-Fan/Investor," TechZone360, May 22, 2012. www.techzone360.com.
Federal Communications Commission	"Spam: Unwanted Text Messages and Email," May 18, 2011. www.fcc.gov.
Jason Gallagher	"Social Media Background Checks Crossing the Line," Yahoo! News, March 24, 2012. http://news.yahoo.com.
Michael Gaul	"Should Employers 'Like' Social Media Background Checks?," Business 2 Community, April 2, 2012. www.business2community.com.
Rebecca Greenfield	"Tweet Goodbye to Your Spambot Followers," *Atlantic*, April 6, 2012.
Mat Honan	"I Flunked My Social Media Background Check. Will You?," *Gizmodo* (blog), July 7, 2011.
Jenny Hope	"Twitter Can Make You Immoral, Claim Scientists," *Mail Online*, April 14, 2009.
Jennifer Preston	"Social Media History Becomes a New Job Hurdle," *New York Times*, July 21, 2011.
Olivia Solon	"Weavrs: The Autonomous, Tweeting Blog-Bots That Feed on Social Content," *Wired*, March 28, 2012.
Tamar Weinberg	"The Ultimate Social Media Etiquette Handbook," *Techipedia* (blog), December 10, 2008.

For Further Discussion

Chapter 1

1. Would Kathleen Cairns agree with Mano Singham that incivility is good for democracy? Why, or why not? How does Cairns's definition of incivility differ from Singham's?

2. After reading the viewpoints by Allison McNeely and danah boyd, do you think that anonymity would encourage you to say things online that you would be unwilling to say while using your real name? If so, would anonymity lead you to greater freedom of speech or to greater incivility, or to both? Explain your answers.

Chapter 2

1. Based on the viewpoints in this chapter, is cyberbullying more or less dangerous than regular bullying? Explain your reasoning.

2. Sameer Hinduja and Justin W. Patchin suggest several things that teachers can do to prevent cyberbullying. Based on the viewpoint by John O. Hayward, could any of Hinduja and Patchin's suggestions be seen as restricting free speech? Explain your answer.

Chapter 3

1. Based on the viewpoints in this chapter, should teen sexting be treated differently than adult sexting? Should there be laws regulating teens who sext, adults who sext, or either? Explain your answers.

2. Based on the viewpoints in this chapter, are online relationships a substitute for real relationships, or are they a way to create new or different real relationships? Explain your reasoning.

Chapter 4

1. What benefits do individuals get from the use of social media? Based on the viewpoints by Kevin Kelleher and PJ Rey, do you think that social media companies exploit users? Explain your answers.

2. Based on the viewpoints by Michael Rainey and *Personnel Today*, do you think that it is unethical or poor etiquette to Google a new acquaintance or a blind date? How would these situations be different from, or similar to, an employer's social background check of an employee? Explain your answers.

Organizations to Contact

The editors have compiled the following list of organizations concerned with the issues debated in this book. The descriptions are derived from materials provided by the organizations. All have publications or information available for interested readers. The list was compiled on the date of publication of the present volume; the information provided here may change. Be aware that many organizations take several weeks or longer to respond to inquiries, so allow as much time as possible.

Alliance Against Fraud (AAF)

National Consumers League, 1701 K Street NW, Suite 1200
Washington, DC 20006
(202) 835-3323 • fax: (202) 835-0747
e-mail: info@nclnet.org
website: www.fraud.org/aaft/aaftinfo.htm

The Alliance Against Fraud (AAF), coordinated by the National Consumers League, is a coalition of public interest groups, trade associations, labor unions, businesses, law enforcement agencies, educators, and consumer protection agencies. AAF members promote efforts to educate the public about telemarketing and Internet fraud, as well as how to shop safely by phone and online. Tips and resources are available on the AAF website.

American Library Association (ALA)

50 E. Huron, Chicago, IL 60611
(800) 545-2433
website: www.ala.org

The American Library Association (ALA) is the oldest and largest library association in the world, with more than sixty-five thousand members. Its mission is to promote the highest quality library and information services, as well as public access to information. ALA offers professional services and publications to members and nonmembers. The association supports the use of social networking sites in libraries and classrooms as a part of economic, cultural, and civic life. Its website includes news updates and fact sheets.

Berkman Center for Internet & Society
23 Everett Street, 2nd Floor, Cambridge, MA   02138
(617) 495-7547 • fax: (617) 495-7641
e-mail: cyber@law.harvard.edu
website: http://cyber.law.harvard.edu

The Berkman Center for Internet & Society conducts research on legal, technical, and social developments in cyberspace as well as assesses the need or lack thereof for laws and sanctions. It publishes a monthly newsletter, *The Filter*, blog posts, and articles based on the center's research efforts. Many of these publications are available on its website, including the final report of the Internet Safety Technical Task Force—*Enhancing Child Safety & Online Technologies*—and "Insights on Cyberbullying: An Interview with a Digital Native," a news report from Berkman's Digital Natives' Reporters in the Field.

Center for Democracy & Technology (CDT)
1634 I Street NW, #1100, Washington, DC   20006
(202) 637-9800 • fax: (202) 637-0968
website: www.cdt.org

The Center for Democracy & Technology (CDT) works to ensure that regulations concerning all current and emerging forms of technology are in accordance with democratic values, especially free expression and privacy. The center works to promote its ideals through research and education, as well as grassroots movements. On its website, CDT publishes articles, reports, and testimony, including "Facebook Age and Anonymity: Civility vs. Freedom of Speech" and "Contrary to Rhetoric: Study Shows Teens Benefit from Use of Pseudonyms."

Electronic Frontier Foundation (EFF)
454 Shotwell Street, San Francisco, CA   94110-1914
(415) 436-9333 • fax: (415) 436-9993

e-mail: information@eff.org
website: www.eff.org

The Electronic Frontier Foundation (EFF) is an organization that aims to promote a better understanding of telecommunications issues. It fosters awareness of civil liberties issues arising from advancements in computer-based communications media and supports litigation to preserve, protect, and extend First Amendment rights in computing and telecommunications technologies. EFF's publications include *Building the Open Road, Crime and Puzzlement,* the quarterly newsletter *Networks & Policy,* the biweekly electronic newsletter *EFFector Online,* and white papers and articles, many of which are available on its website.

Federal Trade Commission (FTC)
600 Pennsylvania Avenue NW, Washington, DC   20580
(202) 326-2222
website: www.ftc.gov

The Federal Trade Commission (FTC) deals with issues of the everyday economic life. It is the only federal agency with both consumer protection and competition jurisdiction. The FTC strives to enforce laws and regulations and to advance consumers' interests by sharing its expertise with federal and state legislatures and US and international government agencies. Publications such as "What Is Phishing?" and "Take Charge: Fighting Back Against Identity Theft" can be downloaded from its website.

Internet Society (ISOC)
1775 Wiehle Avenue, Suite 201, Reston, VA   20190-5108
(703) 439-2120
e-mail: isoc@isoc.org
website: www.isoc.org

A group of technologists, developers, educators, researchers, government representatives, and businesspeople, the Internet Society (ISOC) supports the development and dissemination of standards for the Internet. In addition, it works to ensure global cooperation and coordination for the Internet and related Internet-working technologies and applications. It publishes the bimonthly magazine *On the Internet.*

National Telecommunications and Information Administration (NTIA)
Herbert C. Hoover Building (HCHB)
US Department of Commerce/NTIA
1401 Constitution Avenue NW, Washington, DC 20230
(202) 482-2000
website: www.ntia.doc.gov

The National Telecommunications and Information Administration (NTIA) is an agency in the US Department of Commerce that serves as the executive branch agency principally responsible for advising the president on telecommunications and information policies. In this role, the NTIA frequently works with other executive branch agencies to develop and present the administration's position on these issues. Its offices include the Institute for Telecommunication Sciences (ITS) and the Office of Telecommunications and Information Applications (OTIA).

Pew Internet & American Life Project
1615 L Street NW, Suite 700, Washington, DC 20036
(202) 419-4500 • fax: (202) 419-4505
website: www.pewinternet.org

The Pew Internet & American Life Project is an initiative of the Pew Research Center. The project explores the impact of the Internet on children, families, communities, the workplace, schools, health care, and civic/political life. Pew Internet provides data and analysis on Internet usage and its effects on American society. On its website, the project provides access to articles and reports, including "Twitter Use 2012" and "Older Adults and Internet Use."

WiredSafety
96 Linwood Plaza, #417, Ft. Lee, NJ 07024-3701
(201) 463-8663

e-mail: askparry@wiredsafety.org
website: www.wiredsafety.org

Operating online since 1995, WiredSafety is an Internet patrol organization that not only monitors the web for safety violations but also provides education on all aspects of Internet safety. Volunteers worldwide offer their time and are the driving force of the organization. The WiredSafety website provides information categorized and specialized for parents, educators, law enforcement, and youth; additionally, the website explores topical issues such as social networks, cyberbullying, and sexting. Links to issue- and age-specific projects such as Teenangels, WiredKids, StopCyberbullying, and Internet Super Heroes are also available on the website.

Bibliography of Books

Lori Andrews   *I Know Who You Are and I Saw What You Did: Social Networks and the Death of Privacy*. New York: Free Press, 2012.

Robert J. Cavalier   *The Impact of the Internet on Our Moral Lives*. Albany: State University of New York Press, 2005.

Shawn Marie Edgington   *The Parent's Guide to Texting, Facebook, and Social Media: Understanding the Benefits and Dangers of Parenting in a Digital World*. Dallas, TX: Brown Books, 2011.

Kathy Furgang   *Netiquette: A Student's Guide to Digital Etiquette*. New York: Rosen Central, 2010.

Shane Gibson and Stephen Jagger   *Sociable!: How Social Media Is Turning Sales and Marketing Upside Down*. Charleston, SC: BookSurge Publishing, 2009.

A. David Gordon et al.   *Controversies in Media Ethics*. 3rd ed. New York: Routledge, 2011.

Francis Jacobson Harris   *I Found It on the Internet: Coming of Age Online*. 2nd ed. Chicago, IL: American Library Association, 2011.

Susan Herbst   *Rude Democracy: Civility and Incivility in American Politics*. Philadelphia, PA: Temple University Press, 2010.

Sameer Hinduja and Justin W. Patchin — *School Climate 2.0: Preventing Cyberbullying and Sexting One Classroom at a Time.* Thousand Oaks, CA: Corwin Press, 2012.

Matt Ivester — *Lol . . . OMG!: What Every Student Needs to Know About Online Reputation Management, Digitial Citizenship and Cyberbullying.* Reno, NV: Serra Knight Publishing, 2011.

Thomas A. Jacobs — *Teen Cyberbullying Investigated: Where Do Your Rights End and Consequences Begin?* Minneapolis, MN: Free Spirit Publishing, 2010.

Adam N. Joinson — *Understanding the Psychology of Internet Behaviour: Virtual Worlds, Real Lives.* New York: Palgrave Macmillan, 2003.

Robin M. Kowalski, Susan P. Limber, and Patricia W. Agatston — *Cyberbullying: Bullying in the Digital Age.* 2nd ed. Malden, MA: Wiley-Blackwell, 2012.

Saul Levmore and Martha C. Nussbaum, eds. — *The Offensive Internet: Speech, Privacy, and Reputation.* Cambridge, MA: Harvard University Press, 2010.

Marlene M. Maheu and Rona B. Subotnik — *Infidelity on the Internet: Virtual Relationships and Real Betrayal.* Naperville, IL: Sourcebooks Inc., 2001.

Robert McHale   *Navigating Social Media Legal Risks:*
with Erin Garulay *Safeguarding Your Business.*
                   Indianapolis, IN: Que, 2012.

Brian McWilliams   *Spam Kings: The Real Story Behind*
                   the High-Rolling Hucksters Pushing
                   Porn, Pills, and @*#?% Enlargements.
                   Sebastopol, CA: O'Reilly, 2005.

Sheri Meyers   *Chatting or Cheating: How to Detect*
                   Infidelity, Rebuild Love, and
                   Affair-Proof Your Relationship.
                   Tarzana, CA: From the Heart Media
                   Inc., 2012.

Justin W. Patchin *Cyberbullying Prevention and*
and Sameer   *Response: Expert Perspectives.* New
Hinduja, eds.   York: Routledge, 2012.

Jesse Rice   *The Church of Facebook: How the*
                   Hyperconnected Are Redefining
                   Community. Colorado Springs, CO:
                   David C. Cook, 2009.

Lori Ruff   *#PRIVACY tweet Book01: Addressing*
                   Privacy Concerns in the Day of Social
                   Media. Cupertino, CA: THINKaha,
                   2010.

David Wallace   *One Nation Under Blog: Forget the*
                   Facts . . . Believe What I Say! Dallas,
                   TX: Brown Books Publishing Group,
                   2008.

Laura A. Wankel   *Misbehavior Online in Higher*
and Charles   *Education.* Bingley, UK: Emerald
Wankel, eds.   Group Publishing, 2012.

Nancy E. Willard   *Cyber Savvy: Embracing Digital Safety and Civlity*. Thousand Oaks, CA: Corwin, 2011.

Index

C

CPSIA information can be obtained
at www.ICGtesting.com
Printed in the USA
FFOW021523290313
1047FF

9 780737 764291